Happy Christmas 2004
Love Dinky

NO-DIG GARDENING

HOW TO CREATE AN INSTANT, LOW-MAINTENANCE GARDEN

NO-DIG GARDENING

HOW TO CREATE AN INSTANT, LOW-MAINTENANCE GARDEN

ALLEN GILBERT

ABC
Books

**To my mother, Isobel Fordyce Gilbert,
who did not live to see this book published.**

Published by ABC Books for the
AUSTRALIAN BROADCASTING CORPORATION
GPO Box 9994 Sydney NSW 2001

Copyright © Allen Gilbert and the Australian Broadcasting Corporation 2003

First published April 2003
Reprinted January 2004

All rights reserved. No part of this publication may be reproduced,
stored in a retrieval system or transmitted in any form or by any means,
electronic, mechanical, photocopying, recording or otherwise, without
the prior written permission of the Australian Broadcasting Corporation.

ISBN 0 7333 0941 0

Designed by and typeset by Mega City Design
Illustrations by Nives Porcellato and Andy Craig
All photographs by the author unless otherwise credited
Set in Berkeley $11\frac{1}{2}/14$pt
Colour reproduction by Pageset, Melbourne
Printed and bound in China by Everbest

Contents

	Foreword by Esther Deans OAM	1
	No-dig gardening—an introduction	3
1.	What is no-dig gardening?	5
2.	No-dig garden materials	13
3.	Types of no-dig gardens	23
4.	Planting into no-dig gardens	43
5.	Ongoing maintenance	61
6.	Troubleshooting	67
7.	Educational and community no-dig gardening	81
	Resources	91
	Bibliography	98
	Further reading	101
	Index	103

Foreword

This is primarily a book for all those people who would like to garden but cannot because of monetary, time, physical or space constraints. Even novice gardeners can read this informative book and then create a cheap, instant, easy-weed, no-dig garden that requires very little water and is low maintenance.

Children can also get involved in creating their very own simple gardens and have lots of fun doing it. The book has a full section devoted to ideas for children.

The author describes or provides photographs for more than 50 different ways of gardening without digging. Some of the no-dig gardening ideas will be of particular interest to gardeners with handicaps—who more appropriately should be referred to as 'handicapable'—and those with limited movement or chronic back problems. The gardening ideas described can be carried out with little effort.

This book presents a no-dig gardening alternative for all aspects of gardening, including propagation, landscaping, growing fruit and vegetables organically and using recycled materials in the garden.

I have known and corresponded with the author for more than fifteen years. Allen Gilbert has been involved with presenting educational demonstrations and slide presentations of no-dig gardening methods at garden festivals, garden clubs, local council functions and at educational centres and schools for many years. This is the first comprehensive book to be written in Australia on methods of gardening without digging since the publication of my own book *Esther Deans' Gardening Book: Growing without digging* in 1977.

The book is written in a friendly style and is of particular interest to those who want to grow plants without using chemicals or who want to become partially self-sufficient by growing their own fruits and vegetables. I commend this book as ideal for today's and tomorrow's gardeners and for all those keen gardeners who have not yet begun.

Esther Deans OAM

No-dig gardening–an introduction

No-dig gardening echoes many of the processes in natural forested areas. Forest trees and associated plants rely on continuous recycling of nutrients provided by layers of composting leaves, decaying branches, dying grasses, animal manure, insect frass (excrement and other refuse), bird droppings, dead insects, by-products of fungi and bacteria and dead animals. These provide nutrients for the next generation of forest plants in an enclosed, cyclic ecosystem.

No-dig gardening is an approach to gardening based on a set of simple principles that echo these natural processes. A no-dig garden generally consists of layers of organic material placed directly on the ground. This rots down into a rich layer of compost which is worked on by micro- and macro-organisms to create humus that is nutrient rich, water absorbing and essential for healthy plant growth. Sheet mulching, a method used by many permaculture advocates, is similar to applying no-dig garden layers and also improves the soil in the same way.

Australians were introduced to no-dig gardening in the late 1970s by Esther Deans in her book *Esther Deans' Gardening Book: Growing without digging*. Esther Deans presented the classic method of building an enclosed garden by layering organic materials on the ground, placing animal manure in between the layers and topping the garden bed with compost to complete the no-dig garden. Seedlings and seed were planted in the compost layer and the result was an almost instant garden with no digging involved. Garden edging was made of any number of things including brick, timber, concrete, or any recycled material available.

Since Esther Deans's ground-breaking work, the no-dig gardening concept has spread to encompass many forms of gardening. The traditional, layered no-dig garden has been further developed to include container and pot gardening. Elevated beds have been designed for people with back problems, injuries or disabilities. Innovative gardeners have come up with some interesting ways of growing plants with the idea of conserving energy, water and time spent on weeding.

No-dig gardening has many advantages. It minimises disturbance to the existing soil structure while at the same time improving soil fertility through the addition over time of organic matter rich in nutrients and inhabited by worms, bacteria and fungi. No-dig gardening does not destroy soil structure, as do the mechanical digging operations of rotary hoes or most garden equipment. Soil is stabilised and becomes biologically active, well drained and nutrient rich. This is a particular advantage in most parts of

Australia where many garden soil types are clay based, overworked and generally nutrient poor.

No-dig gardens can be built to any shape or size and be placed anywhere. They can be constructed quickly with a minimum of effort and can be planted on the same day. No digging is required, so no-dig gardens can be built by anyone. For young children, especially, this is a major advantage as they can see the results of their labour and can get to the interesting part of planting without having to go through the long and sometimes tedious process of digging and preparing conventional garden beds. Creating an avenue for children to learn about gardening also allows them to learn how to sustain soils and conserve water and energy and to learn about natural living things; valuable lessons that will prepare them well for the future.

Maintenance of no-dig gardens is minimal because no-dig gardens readily absorb and hold water thus reducing the need to water as often. Weeds are suppressed by the no-dig garden building process so weeding, often a boring and time-consuming task, is minimal.

No-dig gardening has application to wider community involvement in horticulture and agriculture. Demonstrations of no-dig gardening can teach people about recycling, nutrition and organic gardening, and give them an interest in plants. No-dig gardens have been found to be particularly adaptable to community gardening, in housing villages for the elderly and in centres for people with disabilities.

This book outlines some conventional and new ways of making no-dig gardening a success and describes many ways in which gardeners young and old can enjoy easy gardening. All stages of developing a no-dig garden, from building the garden to growing plants from seed and by home propagation, are covered. No-dig gardening can be continued through generations of gardens and the concept of 'generation gardening' and its application to larger areas such as orchards is described. The few problems associated with no-dig gardening are dealt with in Chapter 6: Troubleshooting, together with organic approaches to managing common pests and diseases in no-dig gardens.

1. What is no-dig gardening?

Traditional no-dig gardening is the layering of different organic materials on the soil. In simple terms, the traditional no-dig garden, pioneered by Esther Deans, can be likened to a multi-layered sandwich with many layers of material built into a high, raised garden. Each layer of the garden bed is watered and moistened as the garden is built and the gardens can be built anywhere and to any shape.

The classic no-dig garden is based on a number of simple principles:
- Composting processes
- Composting layers
- The balance between carbon and nitrogen in the materials that make up the compost heap
- Encouragement of soil organisms, particularly worms
- Minimal soil disturbance
- The creation of humus.

Rather than depleting soils as a result of gardening, these principles work together over time to increase soil fertility.

Composting

No-dig gardens are, in effect, composting gardens. The composting process is encouraged by the use of organic materials in layers, the moisture content of the garden bed and the use of fertilisers such as animal manure. A layer of animal manure is placed between every second or third layer of organic material to provide nutrients and to aid in the composting process. The fertiliser provides nutrients to allow nutrient-free materials such as paper, sawdust and wheat straw to break down with the aid of micro-organisms, fungi, bacteria and macro-organisms such as insect larvae and worms.

The effect of a moistened layered system with a good mixture of carbon materials, such as straw, and nitrogen suppliers, like cow manure, is that the whole garden starts to compost and in doing so releases heat and nutrients to the plants growing in the garden. Some materials, such as lucerne and grass clippings, will compost well naturally. These layers need no extra nitrogen to aid composting, but when using grass clippings it is necessary to have thin layers because the material tends to get wet and soggy due to lack of aeration if placed too thickly within the no-dig garden structure. The composting process also breaks down the materials into nutrients that become available for other micro-organisms in the garden such as worms.

The balance between carbon and nitrogen

An important element in the composting process is the balance between carbon and nitrogen—the carbon/nitrogen ratio. No-dig gardens need both high carbon and high nitrogen materials in order to work properly. Nitrogen provides food for micro-organisms and carbon is the material broken down by organisms into compost and humus. Animal manures, grass clippings and green vegetable matter are high in nitrogen while such things as shredded paper, wheat straw, sawdust and chipped wood are high in carbon (see also Chapter 2: No-dig Garden Materials).

Worms and other soil organisms

Worms play an integral role in no-dig gardens, especially where the garden beds are built directly on the ground. Worms drag organic material from the no-dig garden into the soil underneath the garden and in so doing create environments for other soil organisms. The soil structure is greatly improved because of the extra organisms and their by-products of humic acids, detritus and associated bacterial and fungal activity. Worm holes provide aeration vents to pipe oxygen into the soil to create aerobic instead of smelly anaerobic conditions. Improved soil structure allows for better drainage that in turn encourages plants to grow a more fibrous, deep and healthy root system. The plants benefit from this and grow bigger and stronger, able to ward off some pests and diseases. Once a no-dig garden has been 'worked' by worms, the soil underneath the garden—even if it is heavy clay soil—will be vastly improved and more friable. Successive no-dig gardens built on the same spot will gradually improve the soil under the garden to a depth of half a metre or more.

Worms can be added to the no-dig garden or, if the no-dig garden is placed upon soil and has wetted newspaper underneath, worms will tend to invade the garden bed. Worms devour their own weight in plant material and ingested soil particles every day. During the passage of organic material through the worm, the material is concentrated and forms a moist, crumbly end product called vermicast (worm droppings). Worms feed on the materials in the no-dig garden and the vermicast, which is high in nutrients, provides good food for growing plants. Worms, in turn, take organic matter underground into the soil and improve its structure.

Bacteria and fungi also play a part in rotting all the materials into a crumbly compost in which to grow plants.

Minimal soil disturbance

Because no-dig garden beds are built aboveground, less digging into the soil is needed. This minimises physical disturbance with hard-edged digging implements and helps to prevent soil structure deterioration.

Humus

The by-product of organic matter breakdown is humus, which can be described as a gel-like material with the ability to absorb nutrients and moisture. The humus in turn provides nutrients for plant roots and for micro- and macro-organisms within the soil. The activity of these organisms aerates the soil, provides drainage and gives extra nutrients via the by-products they produce.

Increased soil fertility

The classic no-dig garden has many benefits. Apart from being an easy garden to build and to manage, over time it will improve the soil under and around the no-dig garden bed. Some gardeners use a system of patchwork no-dig gardening, where a different square or several squares of soil area are treated to no-dig gardening every year, so that eventually a whole garden area has been covered and, in the process, the soil has been improved. By contrast, in dug gardens the act of physically digging into soil can destroy soil structure, allow the proliferation of weeds and cause drainage run-off with resultant nutrient depletion.

Many gardeners faced with the job of trying to garden in thick, heavy, sticky, muddy clay just give up before they begin. One way to improve clay soils is to add gypsum, lime (if the pH is acidic) and lots of organic matter. Gardens can be built over the heavy clay, without digging at all, following the instructions given later in this chapter for the classic no-dig garden.

If successive no-dig gardens are built on the same spot, the soil structure will be kept at a sustainable level to grow many plants. I have named the act of building successive no-dig gardens on the same spot 'generation gardening'. A second generation garden is built when a second no-dig garden is prepared on the same site as a previous no-dig garden and so on through generations of gardens. Successive gardens can be rebuilt to the original design or just topped up with one or two layers of organic material and fertiliser.

Some vegetables and herbs will self-seed from the first generation garden bed. In successive years, rebuilding need only be of minimum depth to avoid covering the plant stems and so causing stem rot. Deep-rooted plants, such as deciduous fruit trees, can be planted into a second, third or fourth generation garden. By that time the soil has been improved and the no-dig garden materials have been broken down and provide an excellent layer of rich material for planting.

Advantages of no-dig gardening systems

The major advantages of no-dig gardening are that these types of gardens improve the soil, require less work to build and can be built anywhere, anytime, anyhow and to any design. There are, however, many other advantages to no-dig gardening.

- Cleaner vegetables are produced, especially potatoes because there is little or no soil adhering to the skin of the potatoes and they need little washing.
- No-dig gardens are especially good for strawberries, tomatoes and potatoes.
- Continued cropping is allowed. Because of the extra nutrient supply within the garden, no-dig vegetable gardens can be planted with lots of different types of vegetables that mature at different times.
- Companion planting is easily done as no-dig gardening encourages the growing together of different plants.
- There is some evidence that crop rotation needs are reduced because of the build-up of a very biologically active soil medium in which the plants grow.
- The garden soil under no-dig gardens is improved because worms are encouraged to aerate the soil and humus is added to the soil profile.
- Layered or thick no-dig gardens act like a sponge releasing stored water gradually over a long period of time. As

a result they use less water, resulting in reduced water run-off and wastage.
- Building high, well-aerated gardens and planting into the garden edges and sides as well as on top allows a large quantity of crops to be produced in a very small area.
- No-dig gardens require little maintenance and less weeding than conventional garden beds. If weeds do grow they are very easily pulled out of the compost layer.
- Plants are accessible as no-dig beds are usually higher than ordinary garden beds. Vegetables, for example, can be easily harvested. This makes no-dig gardens easy to manage for people with limited movement.
- Portable no-dig gardens can be easily created, as can raised garden beds, again making this type of garden a good one for people who have difficulty gardening conventionally. Portable gardens can be moved around to convenient locations or built to the size and shape that suits particular needs.
- No-dig gardens can be built to provide entertainment and education for children. Because the gardens are built quickly, the interest of children can be sustained and they can see almost instant results from their efforts.
- Many waste products such as animal manures can be used in a no-dig garden and the end product is a reusable compost. Gardening with waste materials is a sensible approach to recycling. In addition, old tyres and other 'junk' can be used to create attractive no-dig garden features.

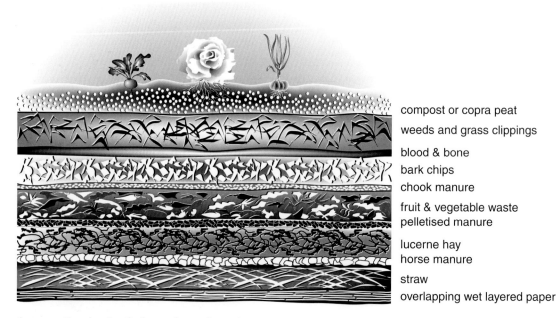

A cross-section showing the layers of a no-dig garden

- compost or copra peat
- weeds and grass clippings
- blood & bone
- bark chips
- chook manure
- fruit & vegetable waste
- pelletised manure
- lucerne hay
- horse manure
- straw
- overlapping wet layered paper

A step-by-step guide to building a simple no-dig garden

With all the advantages in mind, it's time to build a simple no-dig garden based on Esther Deans's classic no-dig garden.

1. Select the site

Begin by deciding on the location and shape of the garden. Basically, the no-dig garden can be built anywhere, even on very poor or heavy soils. If the garden is being built on rock or some other solid surface, it is a good idea to cover the area with small stones, prunings or gravel for aeration before proceeding.

Whatever shape you choose, make the garden bed a good workable size; 1m by 2m is a reasonable and accessible shape. The beds should be narrow enough to allow easy access for weeding or picking produce. Large no-dig gardens may mean carting materials to the site. Smaller gardens will minimise effort and reduce the need for transport of materials.

2. Design the garden

The garden can be structured to have edging made of bricks, poles, timber, mesh or corrugated iron, although edging is not necessary. Recycled timber, bricks, concrete blocks, railway sleepers and hay bales make excellent edging. Some no-dig gardens such as those built with 'pads' from a hay bale are built by interlacing the square-sectioned pads and strengthening all the edges so that the garden wall or edge is self-supporting. A garden shape can also be made using whole bales of hay or other material—if these are fitted together like bricks in a wall, the edging is very solid.

3. Gather the necessary materials

Once you have decided on the site and the design, you need to gather together the materials you will need. To build a simple no-dig garden, you need to have ready the following materials:
- old newspapers;
- a hose connected to a tap, a watering can or some other means of watering;
- compostible materials such as those described in Chapter 2, which deals with no-dig garden materials;
- a variety of good quality seeds or seedlings; and
- suitable edging materials.

4. Put down the base layer of newspaper

The layers of newspaper at the base act as a weed-control measure to prevent persistent weeds growing up through the garden once it is built. Begin by putting a layer of newspaper at the base or on ground level. The newspaper should be

---

Try these alternatives

Alternatives to newspaper include the following.
- Underfelt or non-synthetic carpet: Bill Mollison, author of *Permaculture: A designer's manual*, advocates the use of old carpet underlay to suppress weeds and to recycle materials which might otherwise become part of the waste stream. (Plastic should not be used.)
- Manure or blood and bone placed directly under the paper to provide nutrients for the breakdown of this layer.
- Cardboard is also being used successfully as a base layer in organic no-dig gardens.

interlaced and laid out to the shape needed. Hold down the dry paper with lumps of compost/sand to stop any wind blowing the paper away. Then thoroughly wet the base layer of newspaper. As an alternative, use pre-wetted layers of newspaper.

Although Esther Deans advocates not wetting the paper, we believe it is a good thing to do because if dry layers are used at the base of soil-based no-dig gardens they remain dry and thus the gardener does not have the benefit of biological activity improving the soil structure under the garden. Wetted layers are usually eaten and worked upon by bacteria and fungi and no evidence of the paper will be found after a few months have passed.

5. Add successive layers

Next, add layers of compostible materials (see Chapter 2) to build the garden to the required height. As you place each layer on the garden, wet it with water before adding the next layer. It is important to moisten the layers in the no-dig garden because, like any compost heap, it needs moisture to function properly. Conversely, it must not be too wet or soggy.

Esther Deans suggests that you don't need to water the layers in a shallow no-dig bed. This is true where regular rainfall is experienced, but in very dry areas some watering will have to be done. In gardens that are deeply layered using very dry and/or water repellant materials, such as pressed dry wheat straw from bales, water each layer as the gardens are built, otherwise a dry area may develop at the centre which will be hard to re-wet. Alternatively, pre-wet the dry bales in water or liquid manure for several hours before using them.

Drying out also occurs when materials compost rapidly and are dried out by the heat of composting. Constant examination of the condition of the layers will allow timely watering if it is needed (see Chapter 6: Troubleshooting).

Nearly any type of organic material can be used as a layer in the no-dig garden. It is important to include some layers of materials such as grass clippings or lucerne which are high in nitrogen, or

1. Building a no-dig garden: first, newspaper is laid out in the shape of the garden.

2. Children then place a layer of straw on the garden, while an adult waters the layers.

3. Wetted mashed paper is used as a layer.

4. Compost is shovelled as a top layer onto the self-supporting no-dig garden.

5. Pelletised fertiliser is sprinkled on the garden and water applied to wet the layers.

6. Aerated plastic pipes are used to get extra air into the centre of this large no-dig garden.

7. The top layer is spread on the garden before planting or sowing begins.

8. Finally, the garden is planted and watered.

What is no-dig gardening?

animal manure (pelletised or fresh) as these materials have a good carbon/nitrogen ratio and will start composting readily. High carbon products such as straw, grass, woodchips, cardboard or shredded paper need a nitrogen source to aid in the breakdown of materials. This is why a thin layer of fertiliser between every layer is important.

6. Put down the final layer

The final layer is usually about a 10cm depth of a good, weed-free propagation medium such as mature compost, peat moss or palm peat in which to plant seedlings or sow seeds. An alternative to covering the whole garden area with this last layer is to make holes or 'pockets' in the no-dig garden and place a large handful of compost in each one; seeds, plants or seedlings can be planted into each pocket.

Raised gardens with lots of material may need aeration pipes inserted through the garden to provide extra drainage, prevent waterlogging and help stabilise the garden (see Chapter 6).

7. Plant and fertilise

Once the garden is built and planted, water the plants or seeds with one of the liquid seaweed products to encourage root growth. Further applications of liquid seaweed during the plants' growth will strengthen them and make them more resistant to pests and diseases.

Other types of no-dig gardens are described in Chapter 3, but this simple no-dig garden will give the reader an understanding of the basic steps involved. Once you understand the basic principles, you can try different types of no-dig gardens. Some no-dig gardens are built with one material (for example, compost or manure piles) without layering; others are built in a bag or container containing one material such as potting mix. In most cases, though, the 5–10cm top layer of the garden is usually well-matured compost or other materials such as copra peat or vermiculite.

The range of materials that can be used in a no-dig garden is enormous, as will be seen in the following chapter.

2. No-dig garden materials

No-dig gardens are organic gardens. Layers of organic material act in several ways to save water, reduce heat stress and aid the building up of a biologically active soil. Organisms, such as worms, working in and on the no-dig garden layers, aerate the layers and soil and produce by-products that are rich plant nutrients. Layered materials also inhibit root suckering of plants and allow some roots to grow above heavy soil thus reducing any waterlogging effects. Weeds are controlled and the garden acts as a slow-release watering system. Any plants with shallow fibrous roots will benefit enormously from having mulch around their root systems during the hot summer months.

Most of the materials used to build layers in no-dig gardens are often also used as mulches. Many different types of organic materials are available to use in the construction of a multi-layered or single-layered no-dig garden. Some of these are dealt with in the following sections.

The composting nature of most organic materials means that they will eventually break down into humus. The composting process will break down and degrade many of the polluting materials (such as resins, soap or pesticides) within the mulch. Deep no-dig garden beds can prevent some pests from invading plants and can be used to completely cover the fallen diseased leaves of plants (for example, black spot on rose leaves and apple scab), thus preventing the build-up of diseases. Many of the materials used for no-dig gardens are recycled materials thus preventing excess materials entering the waste stream.

The materials dealt with in this chapter are all suitable for use in layered and other types of no-dig gardens. As discussed in Chapter 1, the balance between carbon and nitrogen in the materials used in the no-dig garden is very important. The following table gives a rough guide to the nitrogen content of the materials listed so that gardeners can achieve a good carbon/nitrogen ratio in their no-dig gardens.

Animal manures Animal droppings are useful for no-dig gardens. If the manure is old or is mixed with a lot of straw, sawdust or other organic material, it can be used as a single-layered no-dig garden. Alternatively, manure can be spread in between each 20–30mm layer.

Common animal manures used by gardeners are fowl, cow, goat, pig, horse and pigeon manures. Duck, guinea pig, aviary, camel, emu, kangaroo, donkey, deer, ostrich and quail manure can be used when available. Zoo animal manure is available packaged as 'Zoo Poo'; although in limited supply, it is very popular. Pelletised animal manures are also available and can be used with mulch materials in no-dig gardens, particularly to supply nitrogen to high carbon, low nitrogen materials such as wheat straw,

Nitrogen content

Industry by-products and recycled waste have not been included in the list as the nitrogen content varies depending on the material.

High	Low	Very low
Animal manures	Brown coal	Bark chips
Bagasse	Compost	Biodynamic straw
Cubed/compressed mulch	Dried citrus peel	Carpet (non-synthetic) and underfelt
'Fish & chips'	Lupin straw	Crop straw
Green manure crops	Mushroom compost	Dried and fresh pine needles
Grass clippings		Eucalypt leaves
Hair		Grape marc
Hydromulch™		Husks and shells
Lucerne		Newspaper
Pasture hay		Palm peat
Pea straw		Paper/cardboard
Sewage waste		Peanut shells
Weeds		Seaweed
Worm castings		Telephone books
		Wool waste

shredded paper, dried grass or sawdust. Manure likely to contain weed seeds is best used as a central layer in the no-dig garden to suppress weed seed germination.

Bagasse is a sugar cane waste product in the form of shredded or pulped sugar cane pieces that have had the syrupy sugar juice extracted by pressing or crushing. The extract contains many nutrients and traces of plant sugar that are beneficial for plant growth and encourage micro-organism activity. Many Queensland organic growers and gardeners use this cheaply available material to great benefit in their gardens.

Bark chips Woodchips, sawdust, wood shavings and mulch from shredding machines can be included in this group. Woodchips contain little nitrogen, but bark and woodchips contain a few nutrients and will rot down readily. Bark and chips from some *Eucalyptus* species (such as river red gum, *E. camaldulensis*, and ironbark, *E. sideroxylon*) and fresh green pine needles contain resins that will inhibit plant growth. Material containing resins will need to be composted for two to three weeks before use in no-dig gardens.

Biodynamic straw Organically and biodynamically grown straw, free of chemicals, is only just becoming available in the marketplace. As more farmers switch to organic methods of growing produce, this material will become more readily available through retail plant nurseries and will be ideal for growing chemical-free food plants in no-dig gardens.

Brown coal While not always readily available to the home gardener, brown coal can be used in soil mixes, propagating mixes, and as topping on no-dig gardens for vegetable seed or seedlings. Brown coal is crumbly, brownish in colour and full of nutrients; however, it is very powdery and cannot be used in thick layers within the garden.

Carpets (non-synthetic) and underfelt Laying old carpet or carpet underlay to suppress weeds or underneath no-dig gardens is a concept popularised by permaculture advocates. This practice is now widely used when establishing gardens and tree plantation areas. The use of carpet underlay is demonstrated at the CERES Centre in Melbourne, Victoria (see the Resources section), where many no-dig garden concepts are also demonstrated.

Compost Any composted material will make a wonderful no-dig garden. It is important, though, that the compost has been made by the hot composting process (see below) so that most weed seeds will be killed and any plant diseases destroyed. Compost that contains weed seeds should be used as an underneath layer in the no-dig garden. Add a layer of a product such as palm peat on top of such compost to exclude light from any weed seed.

Crop straw This refers to the straw left over from harvesting wheat, lupins or oats. The material is low in nitrogen but ideal for no-dig gardens because it does not contain much weed seed. Crop straw bales are usually cheaper to buy than lucerne or pea straw bales. The bales can be used whole as loose straw to create small no-dig gardens or may be broken up into pads which are then spread as layers within the no-dig garden.

Cubed or compressed mulch Pelletised mulch originated from the pelletising of feed material for animals. The pelletised material is less bulky thus saving space

Hot composting

Hot composting refers to the thermophilic (high temperature) stage in the composting process where temperatures rise above 40°C. Temperatures above 60°C for short periods are hot enough to kill most weed seeds and harmful organisms. If the compost heap/material does not have the correct nutrients, moisture and carbon/nitrogen mix, the compost will not get to the hot composting stage and will remain below 40°C. By having all the conditions right, providing extra aeration or turning the heap frequently, hot composting can be made to happen. Many compost heaps are not aerobic, do not get turned and have the wrong mix of materials so they often produce a cool, smelly composting process.

Most books on composting cover the process of hot composting. Two good references are my own book, *No Garbage*, and *Gardening Down Under* by Kevin Handreck.

and allowing extra nutrients to be added per unit area. There are cubed compressed blocks about 20–30mm thick and of various lengths, containing a mixture of beneficial plant food and soil improvement materials, and tubular compressed material about 10mm in diameter of various lengths. These products are mainly comprised of pelletised manures, compost or hay mulch or a mixture of all these materials. When these materials are built into the no-dig garden and wetted, the mulch swells to cover a very large area. Cubed mulch has been tried in above-ground no-dig gardens with great success.

Dried citrus peel Sometimes available as a by-product, citrus peel actually makes a very good no-dig garden layer. Some gardeners cut the peel into small pieces and sun dry the material before use; others cut the peel or put it through a shredder, mix it with many other compost ingredients and compost it before use. Either way works very well.

Dried pine needles/fresh pine needles While fresh pine needles exude a resin that can adversely affect plant growth, dried pine needles can be used and fresh pine needles can be either composted before use or shredded and mixed with a little lime and other materials within a no-dig garden so the resin will not affect plants.

Eucalypt leaves, as a by-product of eucalyptus oil extraction processes, are readily available in huge bales about the size and shape of wool bales. Whole bales of this material can be turned into a no-dig garden.

Unshredded, eucalypt leaves lie flat and become interlaced when used in a no-dig garden. Used without additives such as manure, the leaves will take a very long time to rot down. The slight eucalyptus odour, released when rain occurs or the mulch is wetted, is pleasant in the garden and may assist in regulating or deterring some insect populations.

'Fish & chips' Fish waste from fisheries and waste woodchips from the woodchipping industry are combined and composted into a peat-like texture that is ideal for either layers or topping in no-dig gardens.

Grape marc is the skins and stalks left over after fermentation, filtering and pressing of wine grapes. The material is not commercially available but often can be obtained from wine manufacturers at little cost. Grape marc has some nutritional value and, because it is bulky, can be used to add extra aeration in a no-dig garden.

Grass clippings have an excellent carbon/nitrogen ratio and are readily available to most home gardeners. They can rot or compost quickly without any fertiliser being added, making an ideal layer within a no-dig garden.

If too wet or too thickly spread, grass clippings may compact or form water-resistant layers. This problem can be overcome by mixing the grass with another dry material such as sawdust, autumn leaves or shredded paper. Gardeners sometimes dry the cut grass in the sun before use. Another method is to compost the grass clippings for one to three weeks before use or to use them in one of the lower layers within the no-dig garden.

Green manure crops refer to those crops (such as wheat, oats, clover) that are grown to be ploughed into the soil just before flowering or seed formation. This organic matter adds nutrients and the fibre helps to suppress weed seed germination. Green manure crops can be grown in a no-dig garden then covered with compost or mulch instead of ploughing the material into the soil. To grow a green manure crop, just sow the seed directly on top of the garden, wait until the plants are 20–30cm tall then cover them with a layer of another no-dig garden material.

Hair is organic and will eventually rot down to release all its nutrients into the garden. Hair is rich in micro-elements and a wonderful supplementary plant food to use as a layer in no-dig gardens. It is also one of the preferred foods of worms. However, don't use hair that has been chemically treated.

Husks and shells Food processing and packaging factories discard pods, nut shells, fruit, seeds and flowers of plants and these can all be used for no-dig gardens. This includes almond shells and husks, walnut shells and husks, pecan nut shells, filbert nut shells, peanut shells, pea pods, bean pods, corn cobs, corn cob husks, onion husks, rice hulls, coconut husks and shells, pea waste, coffee grounds, and peach, apricot and nectarine seed and shells. These items are often only available in small quantities, but if gardeners are near a manufacturing or processing outlet they may have free access to large supplies.

Until recently, rice hulls from the processing of wholegrain rice were dumped or burned. Now rice hulls are readily available through plant nursery outlets and although lightweight can be used in combination with other materials in a no-dig garden. Rice hulls can also be used to improve soil structure and aerate the soil because they take a long time to rot down. Black, burnt rice hulls are also available and are used as a soil conditioner.

Walnut shells or peach seed shells will take a long time to degrade into compost so have the added advantage that they will last a long time and improve the structure of the soil or aerate no-dig gardens.

Hydromulch™ This is a liquified mulch containing water, glues, lawn grass seed, Australian native plant seeds (or annual or perennial seeds), fertiliser and chopped straw (or papier-mâché). It is spread onto prepared soil or gardens using high pressure hoses. This is very useful when trying to stabilise embankments, steep slopes and difficult to access areas within the garden area. If annual and perennial seeds are mixed with the mulch, an almost instant cottage garden effect can be obtained by spraying the material onto a no-dig garden. The drawbacks are that this material is relatively expensive for the home gardener and needs to be applied by a contractor.

Industry by-products Waste products from food or plant processing and packaging industries are often available to gardeners. For instance, spent hops, corn husks, asparagus offcuts, pea or bean husks, vegetable waste from greengrocers or fruit waste can all be used as layers or mixed in no-dig gardens. Gardeners should check before using this material to make sure that non-organic products or chemicals have not been added.

Lucerne is an excellent material for building no-dig gardens and was integral to Esther Deans's classic method. It has an excellent carbon/nitrogen ratio and will rot down very easily. Tests by the CSIRO have shown that lucerne straw is particularly good for plants. Often cheap, rain-damaged bales are available to gardeners and these are a good alternative to the usually expensive first-grade bales.

Lupin straw This material is very stalky, weed free, open and well aerated. It rots down quickly and makes a good no-dig garden material. A single bale can be used to create a mini no-dig garden. Although not always readily available, bales can be obtained from some produce stores or directly from farmers.

Mushroom compost When producers finish with mushroom growing media, they package the material for use in home gardens. The pH of this material is usually slightly acid but it can be used in no-dig gardens. The material is relatively cheap, does not smell and is easy to apply. Good quality material should have an endorsement from the Mushroom Growers Association.

Newspaper is a versatile product with many roles in no-dig gardening. Thick layers of newspaper are used as a base for no-dig gardens and shredded or pulverised newspaper can also be used as a layer in no-dig garden beds. Compressed wet newspaper in papier-mâché bricks can also be used as the base layer or as edging. Animal manure or other high nitrogen materials should be placed on top of a layer of newspaper to encourage speedy breakdown.

Palm peat (copra peat) This is a new product available to home gardeners that consists of 100 per cent coconut fibre from old husks and shells. Palm peat is available in the form of compressed bricks about the size of a house brick. Copra peat (palm peat with water added) resembles peat moss and is sold loose in bags. The compressed bricks are easy to use; all you have to do is add water and the material expands to form a loose fibre. Copra peat is also available in wetted form in 30- and 50-litre bags. This weed-free material works very well as a topping layer on no-dig gardens; roots of seedlings and seeds readily grow into it.

Paper sheeting and shredded paper Paper, cardboard (with organic glues) and newspaper can be shredded then used in a no-dig garden, providing animal manure or another high nitrogen material is applied at the same time to initiate the breakdown of the paper. Do not use glossy or highly coloured paper material as this may contain harmful chemical residues that could affect plants.

Pasture hay Bales of pasture hay may contain thousands of weed and grass seeds and must be covered with a weed-free material to exclude light from the seed and prevent it germinating. Fresh green hay can be used as a layer within a no-dig garden. Clover pasture hay contains few viable seeds and can be used just as one very thick layer. Allowing the bales to get wet and partially compost before use will destroy most seeds.

Pea straw This is one of the best materials to use in a no-dig garden. A single bale can be used as a mini no-dig garden. Pea straw breaks down easily, is lightweight and should not contain many weed seeds, although some pea seeds do regenerate.

Peanut shells are a by-product of the peanut industry and are readily available anywhere peanuts are grown, particularly in the peanut growing areas of Queensland. These shells can make an excellent addition to potting mixes, can be used as a mulch, or be used as a thick layer for no-dig gardens. The only drawback is that the shells lose their yellow-brown colour quickly and often grow a natural grey non-pathogenic fungus as they break down.

Recycled waste Many local councils are now providing recycling services for household and garden waste. This material is often shredded and made available to ratepayers at a small cost or may be provided free of charge. It is advisable to hot compost (see earlier) the material before use to kill any harmful seeds or disease organisms. Try using a cubic metre of this material to build a no-dig garden above soil level. Form the material into a garden and add manure through the pile, then plant with potatoes.

Seaweed Beached seaweed can be obtained easily by those gardeners living near the coast and can be used to build no-dig gardens. Seaweed used in small quantities will not need to be washed to remove surface salt but washing is recommended if large amounts are used regularly. Some local councils collect seaweed and compost the waste or take the material to the tip. In some areas, seaweed collection is not allowed so it is wise to check with the local conservation or environmental officer before collecting any seaweed.

Seaweed can be used fresh as a layer or used dry. To dry seaweed, hang it in the sun or other warm, dry place. It can then be broken up into chips and used. Alternatively, seaweed can be placed into a container of water to which some fertiliser is added to create a jelly-like substance

The red carpet treatment

Give yourself the royal red carpet treatment. Lay out an old carpet on all those weeds in the backyard and then slit holes in the carpet where you want to place plants. The carpet should be one that will rot easily and does not contain too many synthetic fibres. A thick layer of organic matter, compost or animal manure can be placed under the carpet to build up the biological activity within the soil. Ask the manufacturer if any poisonous chemicals have been used on the carpets or in their manufacture before laying the carpet in food-producing areas.

that can also be used on no-dig gardens. Some gardeners report extremely good flowering following the use of seaweed as a mulch for flowering plants in no-dig gardens. (Refer to Chapter 5 Ongoing Maintenance for a recipe for homemade seaweed fertiliser.)

Sewage waste This is now becoming more readily available. Sewage waste is being incorporated into soil mixes, mulch products, compost mixes and potting mixes and is sold to gardeners—this material can be used in no-dig gardens. The concern for organic gardeners is the heavy metal content of the material and that long-term use may be detrimental to soils and plants. There is technology being developed to rid the sewage of polluting heavy metals; if this process is effective in removing all pollutants, the use of sewage waste will soon be recommended for gardeners.

In China, and other parts of the world, farmers have been using recycled human waste for many years. Composting toilets allow the use of composted human waste in gardens; however, seek local council advice regarding use of composting toilets in your area.

Telephone books Every year great piles of superseded telephone directories are available. They make excellent recycled materials for no-dig gardens. The books are solid and will not break down easily unless ripped apart or shredded. As complete books, they can be used for edging for no-dig as well as for other types of gardens. Shredded, the books can be mixed with animal manure and used for no-dig gardens. This shredded material is light and will compress, so build the garden bed above the height intended and leave it to rot down for a while. Top the pile with compost and planting can then begin.

An alternative is to mix the shredded paper with materials such as shredded and chipped tree and shrub prunings, that are available as green chipped waste materials from local councils, to add extra nitrogen. Often these materials are supplied free to ratepayers.

Weeds can be used as a layer in the no-dig garden. Some gardeners dry the weeds in the sun for a few days before using or compost them in a plastic bag placed in the sun for two weeks. Alternatively, they can be placed in drums of water to drown. Weeds can also be hot composted (see page 15) or used fresh in the centre of a no-dig garden where light is excluded.

Wool waste such as sheep dags from crutching operations is often readily available in sheep farming areas. Discarded wool can be used to mulch plants, create no-dig gardens, control weeds or to protect plant roots. Untreated wool is full of nutrients and contains natural oils that make it slightly water resistant.

Worm castings (vermicast) One of the easiest ways to recycle kitchen waste and garden waste is to use worm farming to produce vermicast. Vermicast is nature's own fertiliser and can be used as a topping for no-dig gardens. When used as a thin, 20–30mm layer on no-dig gardens, this material out-performs many others as it is a weed-free growing media for the seeds or seedlings planted into the garden and also provides food for the developing plants. Worm castings mixed with other materials such as washed sand can be used for potting and propagation mixes.

Gardeners can buy small worm farm units made commercially by garden supply companies. It is estimated that an average-sized compost bin needs at least 2,000 worms to handle the amount of compost material produced by an average family every day. Worms are easy to handle providing the material they are processing does not become too wet, dry or nutrient poor. The environment around the worms must not get too hot or too cold. Overfeeding is another problem: fed too much, worms can literally swell up and burst. Apart from these problems, the owning or running of a worm farm can be fun for children (and adults), and provide lots of material for no-dig gardens, potting mixes or mulching.

Starting a worm farm

To start a worm farm in a container or compost bin, place 10–20cm of composted material in a mound inside the bin. To this add 1,000–2,000 worms. Place shredded kitchen waste over the dome of compost so that worms have easy access. Material from the kitchen can be added daily in this manner. When the bin becomes nearly full of worm casting, the vermicast material can be removed and spread on the garden or onto clay soil areas to make no-dig gardens or be used as a base or topping.

When vermicast is spread over clay soil, increased biological activity is brought about by the worm castings. The subsequent build-up in worm population, micro-flora and small animals in the soil improves the soil structure and adds organic matter to the soil profile.

3. Types of no-dig gardens

The principle of no-dig gardening can be applied to many forms of gardening to make gardens that require no digging. The classic layered no-dig garden described in Chapter 1 is the traditional form of no-dig gardening, but the principles can be adapted to gardening in various forms, from container gardening to orchard development and maintenance. No-dig gardening can be used for the preparation of lawns, for landscaping the garden or for growing plants in small areas and on balconies, or even for areas inside the home.

Ornamentals, shrubs and trees, annuals and perennials can all be planted in no-dig gardens, and there are some very effective ways to grow vegetables and fruit (as dealt with in Chapter 4: Planting into No-Dig Gardens).

In situ compost gardens

One of the easiest ways to practise no-dig gardening is to use compost. Compost is an ideal material for gardening and can be used in many ways and this is why organic gardening practitioners base their gardening programs on compost production. The most basic of all no-dig gardens is the compost heap used as a garden.

A compost heap ready to be turned into a no-dig garden.

A quick no-dig garden

One of the easiest approaches to no-dig gardening is to grow creepers or groundcovers to cover a given area. Use a thick layer (10–50cm deep) of compost layered on overlapping wetted newspaper. Place the plants in the compost and they will grow vigorously to cover the areas chosen. There are slow-growing and fast-growing creepers and groundcovering plants. Creepers can also be used to make instant topiary shapes. Gardeners must take account of the fact that some creepers will be hard to contain: beware garden escapees that become environmental weeds and do not dump cuttings from creepers such as ivy in the bush.

The compost heap no-dig garden planted and a Hydronurture™ igloo protecting the pumpkin plants.

The simplest compost garden is the one that occurs naturally as a result of the composting process itself. Left alone, layered, open compost heaps have the propensity to gradually rot away, and often heat up during the composting process. If the heating is mild (below 60°C) then many seeds actually benefit from that environment and will germinate. The heating process matures certain seed in the heap and seed from fruit trees and vegetables will germinate and grow from the compost pile.

Some gardeners deliberately 'seed' their compost with such things as a squashed tomato fruit or other plant seed, to ensure some seedlings will grow for next year's cropping. The previous year's vegetables, plants such as tomato, lettuce, potatoes, Jerusalem artichokes, oca, nasturtiums, pumpkins and zucchini marrows, often arise from the 'ashes' of the compost bin. Tomato seedlings raised in these circumstances develop huge fibrous root systems, and are usually very hardy. If the plants are left to mature in the compost, they often produce the best tomatoes in the garden. Plants in the pumpkin family love the slight warmth of the heap and will keep growing if warmth is supplied, even if just to the root system.

Cucurbits (the pumpkin family of plants) need to be kept in continual growth for the full length of the growing season to perform and produce well. The use of water-filled plastic 'tents' or igloos (see Hydronurture™ igloo in the Resources section) will help to give cucurbits a kick-start as well. As compost heap no-dig gardens are usually elevated slightly above the base ground level, extra drainage is supplied and the plants rarely become waterlogged.

An alternative to this natural process is to 'seed' the warm compost heap after it has matured through its heat cycle. A temperature of more than 60°C for 30 minutes will kill most plants and seeds and disease organisms. Seedlings, seeds, potato tubers, or other vegetable plants/seed, and annuals or perennials can be planted and will grow without much attention except for the odd watering that may be necessary. Some gardeners leave the compost in compost bins until it

The compost no-dig garden with mature plants.

matures and then use the bin as a container to grow their plants or vegetables. Many bins are designed in a way that allows this.

Mature compost can also be used to build no-dig gardens on top of the soil, in containers, bathtubs or portable gardens. For compost gardens on top of the soil, the compost material can be spread to the desired depth over the whole area and no-dig gardens can be built so as to improve the soil in those areas. Smaller gardens can be created around the garden area in a random or set pattern to eventually improve the soil in the whole area. Small amounts of pelletised or slow-release organic fertilisers and perhaps a sprinkle of lime can be added before planting any seedlings or seed into the garden. Do not add lime if acid-loving plants such as blueberries or azaleas are to be planted. Plants such as the tomato seem to thrive just on the rich compost without any additional fertiliser. It is important to remember, though, that every time a potted or portable aboveground garden is watered, some of the nutrients are leached out. Light applications of manure or an organic fertiliser monthly or bimonthly during the plants' growing season is good practice for these kinds of compost gardens. The use of misted liquid seaweed foliar applications and root drenches will also be beneficial to all plants.

Compost can also be bagged, tied up or sealed, and the bag used as a no-dig garden. Hessian and canvas bags will rot as the material in the bag composts and can eventually be thrown on the compost heap. Plastic bags can also be used but care must be taken to dispose of the bag separately when the garden is finished with. Drainage holes can be poked in the base of the bag and slits made in the top for planting into. Watering can be done with trickle irrigation, allowing water to drip into the bag at set intervals. Well-aerated compost can be used in piles of tyres to create a vertical garden for the production of crops such as potatoes (see below).

Compost gardens can also be built in old water tanks or half-tanks: tanks with about 1m-high sides or half-tanks are best. Place the tank in a position in the garden where it will receive lots of sunlight. Make sure the base has enough drainage holes in the bottom—a hole of about 10cm diameter placed about every 50cm will suffice. Throw in all garden waste such as weeds, kitchen waste, grass cuttings and mulched prunings and let them rot down. Use animal manure or pelletised animal manure to provide extra nitrogen together with a sprinkle of lime and mineral fertiliser. Fill the tank to overflowing to allow for the volume reduction of organic material as it composts. Add a layer of fresh green grass clippings over the top of the garden area to hasten composting.

During the process the material rots and composts, allowing worms into the tank from the soil on which the tank sits. As an alternative, add worms to the container. Allow the material in the bin to rot down completely for about six months or more then place a layer of completed compost, soil or palm peat or peat moss over the top to plant into. This may be unnecessary if the resulting compost material in the bin has a good crumbly

An easy greenhouse

By covering the half-tank with a plastic dome, the tank can also be converted into a mini greenhouse. Use pliable plastic piping for the superstructure then place one or two layers of clear plastic sheeting over the garden area. The plastic sheet edges can be rolled up during warm weather or to provide aeration. Two layers of plastic insulated with an air gap of 3–5cm will ensure the trapped heat remains inside the greenhouse and provide a warm microclimate for early vegetable production in cool areas.

consistency, allowing the planting of seeds and seedlings straight into the mix. Netting covers can be placed over the young seedlings or germinating seed to prevent birds damaging the plants.

Compost gardens in tanks are particularly suited to areas where rabbits are a problem in the garden. The tanks give the vegetables a certain amount of wind protection, and the metal tank material absorbs heat, warming the growing media and helping the plants along.

Many creeping or climbing plants such as cucumbers, chokos, nasturtiums and pumpkins will grow out of the tank area. Climbing structures can also be built over the tank to give them support. Plant a variety of plants in these gardens to allow companion planting and multiple cropping; produce from the garden can be harvested over a longer time period.

The tanks can be moved from one place to another each season and should be emptied and filled with new material every year to prevent disease and pest build-up. The old compost material can be used to top up or create new vegetable beds or it can just be spread around the garden.

Free heat

Compost in the initial stages of heating/breaking down can be used to provide warmth to seeds and seedlings. Place fresh grass clippings in a polystyrene fruit box to about three-quarters full. Add some well-composted material for a top layer and plant seeds into this. Put a plate of glass or a layer of bubblewrap on top of the box to provide light and keep heat in; lift it to provide ventilation during hot weather. The heating compost provides free heat to the seedlings and initiates germination. The heat retained in the box allows plant growth to continue until the young plants are large enough to plant out into garden beds or into pots.

Portable pyramid

One clever gardener made a no-dig system using a portable, metal, square-based pyramid with the top section removed. The metal was painted black to absorb heat and then a barrow load of grass clippings and a handful of animal manure was placed in it. This was repeated every time the compost cooled. Boards were laid across the open top end of the pyramid and trays of seeds/seedlings, placed on the boards. The heating compost channelled heat up to the base of the seeds or seedlings in the trays, providing an excellent propagation environment using waste materials. The finished compost can be placed back into the vegetable garden.

Esther Deans with a hay bale no-dig garden and 'volunteer' potato crop.

Timber is just one of the materials you can use as an edging for a no-dig garden.

This large no-dig garden features untreated timber edging.

This hip-high no-dig garden is ideal for people with back problems or disabilities.

Portable no-dig gardens like this one are very easy to create.

Ella proudly displays her no-dig gardening produce.

Building a no-dig garden is entertaining and educational for children and adults alike.

Fully productive, small no-dig vegetable garden suitable for small areas.

A quick and easy no-dig garden can be made from a bag of potting mix.

Cubed mulch is very suitable for no-dig gardens.

Recycled carpet can be used around fruit trees; a layer of dried grass clippings adds extra mulch.

A no-dig garden with a dark vermicast layer and compost (light) as a topping.

Worms and vermicast from a small worm farm—vermicast is known as nature's own fertiliser.

Creeping nasturtium and salad greens growing in a no-dig garden.

Compost can also be used for propagation.

Gardeners who have access to large composted piles of manure from cows, horses or fowl can easily create no-dig gardens. This material can simply be made into a pile and the natural composting process will produce some rogue seedlings. Alternatively, the manure can be levelled out and seedlings or seeds planted into it. High piles make ideal gardens for pumpkins and marrows, watermelons and strawberries, and leafy crops such as cabbage and lettuce add to the productivity of the garden and also provide companion plants.

Water-saving gardens

Gardeners living in dry climates with limited supplies of water face a problem when trying to design a garden. No-dig gardening systems lend themselves to these kinds of situations. As well as improving the soil, they reduce water use and insulate the soil underneath from extreme temperatures and from drying out in very dry conditions. No-dig gardens, by their very nature, absorb and retain moisture, which can be delivered to plants over a long period of time thus saving on water use. The gardens need less watering so that run-off and pollution are reduced.

No-dig gardens in dry climate areas, especially those built on the ground, will vastly improve the soil underneath the garden, adding organic matter and over time improving its fertility. The activity of worms, fungi and other organisms ensures that the soil becomes biologically active.

No-dig gravel gardens

Gravel gardens are becoming more popular, particularly as they are suitable for small gardens and require minimal upkeep. All kinds of plants can be planted in gravel gardens, but the usual plants chosen are those that require less water, such as cacti and succulents.

To create a no-dig gravel garden, build a shallow-layered garden that will rot down, then lay paper or cardboard over the area to seal it off. Spread gravel, scoria stones or other inert materials on top of the paper or cardboard to the depth required

---

Create a cactus garden— or a lunar landscape

Spread a 10–20cm sand layer on top of layers of newspaper. Plant the chosen cacti plants into the sand layer; they will thrive in arid areas. Be warned that after 10–20 years some of the beautiful small cacti species may become very large prickly giants. Some protection of the plants may be needed in wet weather to avoid waterlogging. Small-growing cacti can also be grown in large, shallow, plate-like pots for an excellent display.

A gardener from Horsham in Victoria came up with the ideal no-dig rock garden. He placed loads of gravel on the bed then imported different-sized, lichen-covered rocks and placed these so as to create an almost lunar effect. This garden needed no watering or maintenance at all. A variation on the bare rock garden is the Japanese raked sand garden, which can look quite spectacular.

and plant cacti, succulents or hardy Australian native plants into the gravel media. Use rocks to create space and landscape effects and plants in pots to provide colour, foliage or food.

Any cool, damp spot in the garden covered with gravel and rocks will attract moss and create an attractive feature. Encourage moss by spreading a thin layer of good compost over the chosen site and embedding pieces of moss into the substrate. Paint sandy bricks or weathered rocks with substances such as cow's milk, or drench them with liquid seaweed, to provide tiny amounts of nutrition. Then lay pieces of dried moss on the brick surface to encourage the moss spoors to germinate and grow. Given the right conditions of constant moisture, high humidity and shelter from direct sunlight, the patches of moss will grow and grow to carpet large areas.

Some of the alpine Australian native plants can be used in gravel gardens. Pincushion plant (*Scleranthus biflorus*) is a spreading, very low-growing, thickly thatched plant that survives in similar conditions to mosses but is able to withstand hot weather provided it is growing in semi-sheltered positions and given constant moisture. *Scleranthus* plants look like moss when viewed from a distance and can adorn rocks to create a very pleasing bright green patch among gravel and rock formations. The plants can be grown in pots then removed as a layer and placed into position or on rocks within the garden.

Concrete camouflage

Many garden areas have been cemented over either by gardeners tired of the chores associated with gardening or because at one time or another a car parking space was required. Gardeners who purchase houses that have large areas of concrete, rather than digging the whole lot out, can build no-dig gardens on top of the concrete areas.

The no-dig garden will cool the area, by preventing heat absorption and reflection by the concrete. It will also help to prevent excessive drying out of nearby plants. It may be necessary to provide a drainage channel underneath the garden to allow excess water to drain away.

Gardeners can buy segmented concrete hollow squares that are used for placing in driveway areas or along steep banks. The driveway material allows grass to be grown through the concrete to simulate a lawn area but is strong enough to support a car. Partially hollow structural material can also be placed against banks to prevent erosion and creates places for plants. This material is particularly good for hanging and creeping plant species.

Tennis anyone?

An unused tennis court can be turned into a garden with a minimum of effort and without tearing up the surface. Tennis court areas are usually well drained and ideal for placing piles of mulch material or compost to create a no-dig garden landscape. The wire or netted sides can be used for climbing plants or climbing vegetables; the court markings can guide the planting of geometrical designs; or gardeners can create a garden to suit their taste.

Self-seeding gardens

The gaps in between paving stones, bricks or recycled broken concrete paving can offer a haven for weeds, but with a bit of thought gardeners can choose self-seeding plants to grow nearby that spread their seed and have the ability to grow in confined places. All that is needed is to provide a little enriched compost in between the paving layers to encourage seed germination.

Some of the plants suitable for this type of no-dig, self-seeding garden are cosmos (*Cosmos* spp.), mosses (various genus/species), love-in-a-mist (*Nigella damascena*), kiss-me-quick (*Centranthus ruber*), erigeron (*Erigeron* spp.), asters (*Aster* spp.), violets and viola (*Viola* spp.) and alyssum (*Alyssum* spp.). All these plants self-seed or regrow every season to create tufts of plant growth in between the paving. Many perennials send down long, strong root stems and provide a splendid, lengthy display of flowers against a pattern of paving. Some thought must be given to those plants that could become environmental weeds; exclude them if they are a problem in your area.

Gaps in paving act as a refuge for self-sown plants.

Hay and hay bale gardens

Hay bales make an important contribution to no-dig gardening. Hay bales can be broken up and used as a layer in the garden. The pads that comprise the standard hay bale can be used as edging. Left whole, a single hay bale can be converted into an almost instant no-dig garden, or hay bales can be used in multiples—in rows or stacks.

Hay bales are readily available, even in city areas. Sometimes spoiled hay from farmers is available at a very, very cheap rate. Gardeners can take advantage of this.

Gardening with hay bales can be adapted for aboveground elevated gardens and for gardening in small places, on rooftops or in large containers.

Hay bale gardens will benefit from frequent applications of a liquid seaweed product, which will ensure good root growth. Fertiliser or organic pelletised manures can also be added to the growing plants if needed. Tree fertiliser pellets can also be used as they break down slowly and release nutrients gradually over a long period of time. When growing potatoes, more tubers will form if potassium and phosphorous in particular are given to the plants as they mature. The bale gradually rots down during the season, providing mulch for plants such as tomatoes, pumpkins, marrows and strawberries, to name a few that perform well when planted into bales of hay.

As previously mentioned, no-dig gardens can be made from stacked bales of hay as well. One approach is to use layered bales at the base of the garden, with a two to three bale high side edging to protect the garden from wind and cool

An unusual recipe for hay bale potatoes

Soak the hay bale in water to allow further retention of applied nutrients (do this by using plastic sheeting to contain the water around the bale or by dumping the bale into an old bathtub or a dam). After wetting the straw, drench the bale with a bottle of molasses (or alternative), water with a liquid seaweed product then scoop a hole in the bale and place potato tubers in the hole. Cover the tubers with compost or sawdust and watch them grow.

A hay bale no-dig garden planted with potatoes and mulched with mulch cubes—a simple but effective way to grow potatoes.

weather. This garden can also be turned into a makeshift greenhouse (see the section on propagation in Chapter 4). Large bales can be used around the outside of the garden and the centre filled with loose hay and material from broken bales. Both stacked and single hay bale gardens have been used very successfully to grow pumpkins.

To build a multi-layered hay bale no-dig garden, thoroughly wet the bales and place a 5–30mm layer of compost on the top ready for planting. Add a small amount of granular organic fertiliser or pelletised manure to the compost topping at planting or sowing time.

Deep no-dig hay bale gardens need extra aeration as the centre of the gardens may become hostile for plant root growth due to lack of air. Aeration pipes through the garden (as described in Chapter 6 Troubleshooting) will help to supply the extra air needed for plant root or tuber growth and reduce waterlogging.

Another way to use several bales is to make a hollow square-shaped garden with the sides made of hay bales stacked one to three bales high. This area can then be used for a compost heap: place all garden weeds and waste plant material into it then add some animal manure and a layer of green grass clippings on top to aid composting. When this open bin is full, top it up with compost or palm peat and plant it as a no-dig garden. Another way is to bore out the centre of a giant round hay bale to create a hollow. This bale can then be used as a no-dig garden.

My partner and I use hay bale no-dig gardening. We use mixed grass species hay bales cut from our own paddocks. The bales are full of seeds so are left in the open to allow rain to fully wet them. This process causes the bales to compost and become quite hot inside. The partial composting and the continual wetting

Building a no-dig garden compost heap with hay bales.
Step 1: Construct the garden walls.

Step 2: Fill the compost area with selected materials and plant.

Step 3: Watch your crop of potatoes grow!

Portable no-dig gardens for sale

Commercially available, small, baled materials can be used to create instant no-dig gardens for tomatoes. Cut a hole about 30–40cm in the plastic cover and remove the plastic circle. Use a knife to make slits in the base for drainage. Remove a few handfuls of the bale material and put compost in the hole. Then insert a tomato plant or other vegetable seedlings, annuals or perennials into the top of the bale. Add lime to reduce the acidity of the organic material and place organic fertiliser such as blood and bone in a circle around the plants, about 20cm away from the root system to avoid burning. Water the plants with a liquid seaweed preparation and place the bale in a position that receives plenty of sunlight.

A bag of mulch can be used similarly, but a little more fertiliser will be needed to help break down the mulch. If the garden slumps as the mulch composts, extra mulch may have to be pushed into the bag to stabilise the no-dig garden.

kills seeds by heat and by waterlogging. After a few months the hay bales are ready to use in the garden. We use the bales to build three-sided, square-shaped compost enclosures. The inside area is filled with all our weeds and garden refuse, as well as some kitchen waste. Eventually, the compost pile is heaped up above the top bale. At this stage we place a deep, 5–10cm layer of freshly cut grass on top. This encourages further composting.

The compost enclosure tends to produce 'volunteer' plants such as nasturtiums, potatoes, tomatoes, Jerusalem artichokes and oca, but the garden can be deliberately planted with annuals and vegetables once the grass topping has broken down. The sides of the enclosure have been used to propagate plants such as grape vines. The cut, 20–30cm pieces are simply pushed into the moistened hay bales to about half their length and left alone. The rooted cuttings are pulled out of the bale in autumn and transplanted into the garden orchard. After one season of producing vegetables, annuals or perennials, the hay bale compost heap is broken apart and used to form vegetable beds or the rotted hay from the sides is used as mulch around fruit trees.

Grow bag gardens

No-dig gardens can be easily made from bags filled with soil mix, plant media or mature compost. Fill the bags with the material, seal them and lay them flat. Punch holes into the base for drainage. Make cuts with a knife in the top and sides of the bag for planting.

Place plants into the holes or slits on top of the bag. Water the plants by jamming a plastic funnel into the bag as an entry point for watering, drip-feeding or trickle irrigation. Grow bag no-dig gardens are portable and very easy to handle; they can be placed on shelves, above ground, on patios or concrete, on portable tables or in open garden areas. This system is nearly completely weed free and many vegetables, annuals or perennials can be grown in the bags.

Commercial grow bags are available. However, gardeners can make their own vertical hanging grow bags from thick black plastic by sewing narrow pieces into a tube with the base closed and the top open for filling. Place soil mix, potting mix or layers of no-dig garden materials in the bags, cut slits into the sides, and insert plants into these spaces. This type of grow bag is excellent for strawberries.

Grow bag gardens are particularly suited to gardeners with little space because the bags can be hung to take advantage of any space that is not used. If the bags are hung in a small greenhouse, other vegetables or plants can be planted in the soil or in pots under the hanging tubular gardens. Inventive gardeners can have a succession of these sausage-type gardens in the porch, sunroom or even

> ### Productive potato patch
>
> I have turned a lupin hay bale into a no-dig garden and planted black potatoes ('Purple Congo') in it. The hay bale produced twice as many tubers as nearby open-ground grown potatoes; and, of course, they were clean and easy to harvest compared to the potatoes grown in the soil.

inside the house, providing a drip tray is hung underneath the gardens to collect run-off from fertiliser and watering applications.

Potato systems

Potatoes are an excellent starter for gardens in difficult areas with poor soil. All you need to do is spread gypsum and lime then a layer of newspaper (at least eight pages thickness) as per the classic no-dig garden described in Chapter 1. Then place potato tubers on the paper or in holes cut through the paper at selected intervals. Finally, cover the tubers with piles of compost or layers of weed seed free hay (for example, lupin, wheat, pea or oat straw or lucerne hay).

As the plants grow, nutrients must be supplied: nitrogen in the early stages for growth, and potassium and phosphorus in the latter stages for the production of tubers. There are many organic liquid fertilisers that can also be used as foliar sprays as the plants grow to enhance production. Many gardeners just rely on rich compost to supply all the nutrients needed by the potatoes.

As the plants grow, add extra layers of compost or hay, allowing about 30–50cm of green plant growth to remain above the layer of mulch material. A fertiliser rich in phosphorus and potassium can be added with each successive layer of compost or hay. If the area being used is boxed in, the hay/compost can be built up to the top of the construction.

The material used to cover the potatoes does not have to be hay. Chipped mulch from local councils, grass clippings, lucerne, lupin trash, pea straw, sawdust (excluding green sawdust from treated wood), autumn leaves, shredded paper or any readily available organic material will do (see Chapter 2). A mixed layer system will also work effectively.

Potatoes can be harvested at the end of the season or, alternatively, as they become large enough to eat—a process called 'bandicooting' by some Australian gardeners. By the time the potatoes are harvested, the underground paper will have rotted, some tubers will have grown into the soil, worms will have entered the

> ### Alternatives to grass
>
> An alternative to lawns planted with grass is the use of creepers that will eventually cover a large area. Lippia (*Phyla nodiflora*) or black coral pea (*Kennedia nigricans*) are good plants for this. Lawn chamomile (*Chamaemelum nobile*) is a pleasant smelling alternative to the usual grass lawn. Both of these options can be planted using the no-dig techniques described. They are not, however, suitable for high usage areas.

> ### Quick and easy topiary
>
> Commercially available lawn grass can be wrapped around a set-shaped hessian base to create instant topiary. Or glue grass seed (together with some materials such as pulp paper and fertiliser) to the hessian: the grass seeds will sprout once watered. Many designers have created unusual topiary shapes, such as dragons with grass skin and cars with grassy paint, for use in shows or to be used as garden and parkland ornaments.

area and aerated the soil, and the humus and nutrients from the no-dig garden will have leached into the soil profile. Organic macro- and micro-organisms, fungi and bacteria will have proliferated in the area under the garden, conditioning the soil. The area will be suitable for the next generation no-dig garden and for other plantings.

No-dig lawns

Even lawns can be created without digging. There are several ways to do this.

Using rolled-strip lawn material is the easiest way. Choose any area for the instant lawn, provided plenty of sunlight penetrates to the grassed area. Cover an existing grass or weedy area with wetted newspaper and spread a layer of sifted

Potatoes in tyres

To grow potatoes in tyres, place one tyre on the ground (or patio, garden bed, brick area or rooftop) and fill it with soil or compost. Mix in some rock phosphate, a small amount of animal manure and a handful of lime. Place two to four potato tubers in the compost, water with liquid seaweed to encourage root formation, and allow the plants to grow.

When the plants are 30–50cm above the top of the tyre, an extra tyre can be added and more compost placed around the growing plant. About 20cm of potato plant growth must be above the topmost tyre at all times, so the plant can convert sunlight into food and continue to grow unimpeded.

As the layers of compost are added, sprinkle a handful of potash and phosphorous fertiliser onto the compost layer to encourage tuber formation. Liquid fertilisers could also be used as foliar applications during the growth of the potato plants. Regular liquid seaweed foliar sprays on potatoes produce larger crops albeit with slightly smaller but even-sized tubers.

Beware of rats and mice. Mice, especially, have a habit of making the tyre stack into a multi-storey apartment block; they love to eat the small immature tubers and can destroy all your good work.

Potatoes planted in a tyre tier.

Potatoes growing in piled tyres.

mature compost or soil mix on top of this. Lay strips of the instant lawn on the compost/soil and roll them into place for an instant no-dig lawn. Make sure that the base of the instant turf is firmly in contact with the soil or compost layer underneath —any air gap between these two interfaces will kill the roots of the grass.

Another method is to use hessian as a garden base. Glue the grass seed onto the surface of the hessian with an organic glue (a simple flour and water glue will do) and layer the hessian onto an area; keep it moist. The hessian also prevents soil erosion when attached to soil on sloping banks. Alternatively, build a shallow-layered no-dig garden that will rot down and lay the hessian on top.

Recycled paper in the form of a papier-mâché slurry mixed with lawn seed or plant seed, glue and a small amount of fertiliser can be sprayed onto lawn areas. This material sets to form an elastic skin on the garden bed or lawn area that kills weeds by excluding light. The plants (for example, Australian flora seed) or lawn seed germinate and grow, giving the gardener an easy (although fairly expensive) way of forming an instant landscape without any digging at all.

Products are available containing a mixture of papier-mâché, some fertiliser and lawn seed. All you have to do is spread the mix on the bare area within the lawn to patch up the holes left by weeding, etc. After watering, the seeds germinate and instant patching occurs within days.

Tyre gardens

Tyres make great no-dig gardens suitable for all kinds of plants. There are more than 17 million worn tyres thrown away by motorists in Australia each year. Some of these can be saved for recycling into tyre-formed no-dig gardens. Giant tyres from earthmoving equipment make especially good containers for no-dig gardens. The tyres can be cut in half and placed together side by side to form a trough, or laid one upon the other to form a vertical garden. Layers of tyres can also been used to shore up earth and build terraced no-dig gardens on sloping areas. The tyres can be laced together to provide extra strength and the inside of the tyres filled with earth to stabilise the slope, then the no-dig garden can be built behind this support. There are several variations of swan designs of cut tyres used as planters; tyres are cut and formed into the shape of a swan, painted appropriately and then planted.

Tyre gardens are excellent for growing potatoes as they can be built up into tiers as the potato plants develop. It is important that the filling used in the tyres is a lightweight material such as compost because heavy materials such as clay or sand will squeeze the developing root tubers and inhibit their formation, especially if the column of tyres is more than 1m tall.

Other plants suitable for small tyre gardens containing one to four fixed tyre layers are silver beet, onion, tomato, sweet potato, pumpkin and lettuce.

Excellent garden containers or planters can also be made from old tyres still on the tyre rim and a short axle or support. Cut through the tyre at one side of the tread then roll back the tread piece and push it upwards to create a saucer-shaped

New boots from old

Old boots can be spruced up with polish or paint and used as potted plant holders. Old leather boots add an old-world style to the garden, patio or porch. Gumboots can be planted and the black rubber painted to conform to your own colour scheme. Try attaching string or wire to the gumboots to make hanging gardens. Punch holes into the sides of the gumboots to make pockets for planting annuals, herbs or strawberries.

Old boots transformed into no-dig garden ornaments.

container. Weld the rim to a support or use an old axle to create a turntable-like garden.

Drill drainage holes in the tyre to allow for proper drainage. Fill the tyre area with compost then plant herbs, annuals, perennials, vegetables, creeping plants such as campanula or Serbian bellflower (*Campanula poscharskyana*) or strawberries (*Fragaria* spp.). The container can be painted to add extra colour to the garden; it is durable and reasonably portable.

Cottage gardens

Once established, cottage gardens become, in effect, no-dig gardens. The close-planted annuals and perennials typical of the cottage garden can be allowed to self-seed every year to provide continuous displays. To begin a no-dig cottage garden, layer newspaper onto the soil or grassed

Feature gardens

Old stumps make great feature gardens. There are many ingenious ways to use old trees, old stumps, branches or saw log offcuts (pieces trimmed from saw logs). Hanging hollow stumps can substitute for hanging baskets. Hollowed out logs are ideal for trough gardens. Used sleeper offcuts can be used to build the sides of no-dig gardens and bark can be used to make the layers of no-dig gardens. Tree stumps can also be sculptured into statues to suit the garden landscape.

Stumps can easily be turned into a landscape feature by placing hanging basket pots all around the limbs or by planting (in a pile of compost at the base of the stump) fast-growing creepers such as honeysuckle (*Lonicera* spp.), passion flowers including passionfruit (*Passiflora* spp.), wisteria (*Wisteria* spp.), Chinese gooseberry or kiwifruit (*Actinidia deliciosa*), wonga wonga vine and bower vine (*Pandorea* spp.), bougainvillea (*Bougainvillea* spp.) or sweet-smelling jasmine (*Jasminum* spp.).

Unusual pots

To provide variety, gardeners should not have to stick to conventional pots. Recycled containers can add new dimensions to gardening design: half wine barrels, old fruit box containers, boots or washing tubs can be used to create a wonderful cottage garden effect. Any old equipment with troughs or trays can be filled with potted plants for extra visual effect. Plants can be kept in their own pots and grouped together for good effect, or the plants can be planted out, depending on the type of container.

An old teapot and potty turned into no-dig garden ornaments.

Tithonia plants in a barrow make a great no-dig garden ornament.

A sculpture made into a hanging no-dig garden.

A half wine barrel no-dig garden.

Types of no-dig gardens **37**

area then add layers of clean straw, lucerne straw, chipped mulch or other materials (see Chapter 2). Add fertiliser and let the material compost then plant the seedlings into this layer. Place a handful of compost at the base of each seedling to help it to get established and water the seedling with a liquid seaweed product. Seed, on the other hand, can be sown into the garden by sprinkling it on the top of the prepared garden area. Seeds will eventually germinate and provide plants. These can be nurtured early on and cut back during the autumn–winter period; they then require very little maintenance.

The same principle can be applied to various vegetable plants such as the perennial lettuce, some radishes, carrots, parsnip, silver beet and swede. Just allow one or two plants to go to seed and the seedlings will regenerate the following year.

Plants in cottage gardens will need to be regularly topped up with extra layers of material. Where perennials that die down annually or bulbs are grown, thick no-dig layers can be reapplied yearly. However, if small plants are still actively growing or seedlings are beginning to grow, only a thin layer can be applied otherwise stem rot may occur. Volunteer seedlings from self-seeding plants and those that arise in the no-dig orchard will have to be thinned to prevent overcrowding and dwarfing of the plants due to competition for nutrients, water and light. Seedlings that are culled can be transferred to other no-dig garden areas or swapped with friends.

Cottage garden effects can be enhanced by the use of old containers or railway sleepers. Innovative gardeners can buy variously designed bins, some of which are portable, and use these as plant containers. Recycled or new pipes made from concrete, terracotta or other materials are ideal for cutting into different lengths and standing vertically. The pipes can be filled by layering materials as in the simple no-dig garden or with potting mix, compost or a potting media, but allowance must be made for free drainage from the base of the open

Potted pincushions

Several plants that have a mat-type growth can look spectacular in pots or other vessels. The best in this group are pincushion plant (*Scleranthus biflorus*), baby's tears (*Soleirolia soleirolii*), pratia (*Pratia pedunculata*) and creeping boobialla (*Myoporum parvifolium*).

Hanging gardens

The fuchsia is one of the many plants with some semi-weeping forms that can, with constant tip-pruning, give a beautifully shaped plant. Some others that give spectacular displays in hanging baskets are: roses, blue plumbago (*Plumbago auriculata*), plectranthus (*Plectranthus* spp.), pelargonium (*Pelargonium* spp.), lantana (*Lantana* spp.; note, though, that this may become a weed in some areas), purple velvet plant (*Gynura aurantiaca*), kangaroo vine (*Cissus antarctica*), shrimp plant (*Justicia brandegeana*), bougainvillea (*Bougainvillea* spp.), paper daisies or strawflowers (e.g. *Rhodanthe* spp.) and blue leschenaultia (e.g. *Leschenaultia biloba*).

> ### Trailing plants for baskets
>
> Trailing plants that do well in hanging baskets are those species which in their natural environment would be creeping plants, such as: piggy-back plant (*Tolmiea menziesii*), strawberries (*Fragaria* spp.), spider plant (*Chlorophytum comosum*), ivy (*Hedera* spp.; note, though, that this needs to be carefully managed to avoid it becoming a weed), and succulents such as chain of hearts (*Ceropegia linearis* subsp. *woodii*) and donkey's tail (*Sedum morganianum*).

ended pipes. All types of plants can be grown but creeping or hanging plants (for example, strawberries) work very well and look particularly attractive.

Old farmyard machinery can be used to effect in a cottage garden. It may be necessary to clean the machinery or paint it so that further deterioration is minimised, but no digging is involved. Old mowers, cream cans, metal spoked wheels, wooden wheels, old horse-drawn carts, factory machinery—all can give an interesting design aspect to the garden. Old household items can be used to create no-dig container gardens. In the course of one year, most gardeners will throw away at least one pair of old shoes or boots—rather than being thrown away they can be transformed into interesting ornament within the garden.

Pots of various kinds add another dimension to the garden, as do hanging baskets. All you need are pots, plants (or seed), bags of compost or soil mix and some way of watering the plants. Self-watering pots are of great advantage in saving time and reducing watering needs.

Hanging baskets located on the verandah of a cottage garden add effect from inside the house as well as outside. They can also be used to cover a wall, hang on fences or decorate a shady tree.

Preparing hanging baskets involves choices about the most appropriate container and about the soil/medium to be used, as well as about the type of plants. Some gardeners choose any old pot and by selective planting make that pot attractive; others select the plant then choose a complementary pot.

Some bulbs look really good in hanging baskets. In general, the best bulbs for hanging baskets are the small-growing types which include: oxalis (*Oxalis hirta*), rose grass (*Rhodohypoxis baurii*), hoop-petticoat daffodils (*Narcissus bulbocodium*), grape hyacinth (*Muscari* spp.), freesia (*Freesia* spp. and hybrids), and baboon flower (*Babiana stricta* and hybrids). Some bulbs look great in large pots, especially elephant's ears (*Colocasia esculenta*), belladonna lily or naked lady (*Amaryllis belladonna*), Cuban lily (*Scilla peruviana*), pineapple lily (*Eucomis comosa*) and forest lily (*Veltheimia bracteata*).

The no-dig orchard

If you want to grow your own fruit but don't want to buy grafted trees because of the cost involved, or don't want to be hassled with site and soil preparation, try the no-dig approach.

Ideally, the orchard site should be well drained, have good soil and receive plenty of sunlight. The area should be sheltered from strong winds and be relatively free of frost. If the site is near a fence or building in a very small area, then the orchard can

> **Easy orchards**
>
> A gardener in Tongala, Victoria, tried the no-dig orchard system and within three years obtained good crops of apricots, peaches and nectarines. The orchard includes different varieties that mature at different times, so very little thinning of the seedling trees has to be done. Fresh fruit can now be picked from that orchard over a long period of time.
>
>
>
> A no-dig orchard area created by planting seeds in compost.

still be planted and the trees trained to a space-saving espalier system.

Once the site has been selected, build a layered no-dig garden. This can be seeded with fruit waste containing seeds or used as a vegetable garden area to begin with. Once second and successive no-dig garden areas have been built, the area will have increased in fertility and be ready for planting with commercially available bare-rooted fruit trees or rootstock.

It is not necessary to buy fruit trees, however, as it is easy to germinate orchard species in the no-dig garden. All you have to do is pick a slight depression in the soil for the site then heap fruit waste and compost material into the area. Covering the compost material with mature compost or well-drained soil will help the seeds in the waste to germinate.

Germinating seeds of common fruits and nuts such as peach, nectarine, apricot, plum, hazelnut, almond and walnut need the seed coat to break down before the seed kernel starts to grow—this will happen in a year or so in compost and often more quickly.

Unlike apple and pear seeds, the *Prunus* family (for example, plum, apricot, nectarine, peach and almond) will usually grow trees that will bear acceptable fruits, although nuts take a while to mature and grafting the seedling may seem a good alternative. Nectarines almost always produce good quality fruit from seedling trees. Plums are very varied: they could be red fleshed, yellow fleshed, large, or small fruits with different coloured skins, but they do produce edible fruits. Apricots will produce good fruit on seedling trees in about 60 per cent of cases; nectarines and peaches produce good fruits in about 95 per cent of seedlings. Unfortunately, apples only have about a 40 per cent chance of producing good fruits and pears about a 10 per cent chance.

It is important not to prune plum and apricot seedlings until they fruit. Peaches and nectarines will take about one to three years to produce fruits, plums three to five if left unpruned, and apricots three to seven, again if left unpruned. Pruning of strong-growing seedling trees actually promotes growth and juvenility and the seedlings may take many years to slow down growth to begin fruiting. Conversely, if seedlings are well pruned, the strong new lateral branches could be used to create a multi-grafted tree with lots of different cultivars or one type on the one tree.

As an alternative method of developing the no-dig seedling tree orchard, gardeners can grow any seedling (including citrus, apple and pear) and use it as rootstock on which to graft many varieties. A grafted 'fruit salad' tree could be part of the orchard, with all types of citrus plants; or grow another with various stone fruit (peach, nectarine, plum, prune, apricot, almond); or grow a pome fruit (apple, pear, medlar, quince) tree.

Portable no-dig gardens

No-dig gardening systems can be adapted to make them portable—a boon for people who have difficulty bending or reaching gardens at ground level. There are several ways of making portable no-dig gardens, including some of those already mentioned: hay bales, pots, bags and bathtubs. Portable gardens made to order are also available. These are usually of simple construction and are above ground to enable wheelchair access, sometimes with wheels for easy relocation. Some areas at the Kevin Heinze Garden Centre in Melbourne (see the Resources section) have been made into rotating hanging basket form to save space and allow easy access.

Water gardens

Water gardens of various sorts can be considered another form of no-dig gardening, especially if the water garden uses recycled materials. Water will attract wildlife, frogs and birds, and become a breeding ground for predator insects such as the dragonfly. It will also provide humidity to that area of the garden. It can be relaxing just to sit and look at a body of water and the sound of running water adds to the atmosphere of any garden. Water features provide a haven for dwindling frog species, and the sounds of frogs at night add another element to the garden landscape.

When constructing ponds, most gardeners dig into the soil to hollow out a depression. However, there are alternatives that require little or no digging or earth removal. Many gardens already have dips, holes or depressions that can easily be turned into a pond area for the growing of water plants. Place waste dirt or topsoil on the ground to build banks for the construction of a pool.

Bathtub frog pond

Place an old bathtub under trees for some shelter and shade. Position the tub where it will still collect rainwater. Make sure that a good plug is in the base, fill the tub with water from a dam and include some of the small life forms, such as swimmers, found there. Obtain a floating aquatic plant such as *Azolla filiculoides* to float on top of the water to provide protection and water aeration. Introduce some tadpoles and allow the life forms to adapt to the new environment. Placing a few old leaves and twigs in the tub may also be beneficial for tadpole survival. By preparing the tub in this fashion, you may find that the population of tadpoles suddenly increases. This is because frogs are attracted to the 'frog pond' and lay more eggs that then hatch into many more tadpoles.

Spread special rubberised or thick plastic sheeting over the area to form the pond base. Cover the edges of the sheet and place rocks or bricks or other material around the edges to create a natural look. After filling the pond with water, submerge plants such as water lilies in pots by placing them on the bottom of the pond. Add artefacts, statues, ferns and other plants or fish to create a special no-dig pond landscape area.

Every year, housing renovations create junk. Among the junk often thrown on tip sites are thousands of old bathtubs. Bathtubs are ideal for no-dig gardening. They have a ready-made drainage point, are protected on the sides and create an interesting effect when used as water gardens or as tubs for no-dig gardening. The tubs can be reinstalled in the house as an indoor garden, used outside, or placed on balconies, porches or verandah areas. Bathtubs can be used as a water garden or pond or for growing water-loving vegetables such as watercress or lotus root.

This compost bin was turned into a no-dig garden after the compost matured.

A tomato plant flourishes in a no-dig garden made with pure mushroom waste.

A large area of no-dig gardens built to improve the soil.

The preparation of a half-tank no-dig garden, with a topping of green grass clippings to speed up composting.

Successful half-tank no-dig gardens.

A square pyramid container heated by compost for propagation purposes.

To encourage the growth of moss, place some rocks in a cool, damp spot in the garden, paint them with cow's milk or liquid seaweed then lay pieces of dried moss on them.

An easily prepared cacti no-dig garden.

A commercial hanging bag container with violas in flower—ideal for no-dig gardening.

This homemade hanging bag using plastic sheeting and wire mesh is great for growing strawberry plants.

This illusion garden was created in a 1-metre space and would be suitable for the wall or fence of an old tennis court. (Courtesy GH Butters and Associates)

A homemade, grow bag, no-dig garden using a recycled jute bag and compost filling, planted with capsicums.

Clean 'Bison' potatoes from a no-dig garden.

4. Planting into no-dig gardens

Plants growing in the wild do not rely on humans to plant them or look after them but have evolved systems of reproduction based on natural mulch and sometimes animal fertilisers or animal digestive tracts to help to germinate seeds. The mulch on the earth is the crucial factor in allowing seeds to grow, while earthworms and other animals work the soil to make it a friable structure suitable for growing plants and seedlings. In the natural environment, all annuals and perennials survive mostly by relying on composted mulch on the soil. Even crevices on mountains will grow plants and trees if accumulated airborne dust, debri and plant leaves have lodged in a depression where a plant can grow.

No-dig gardening in many ways simulates these natural conditions through prepared layered garden beds that offer adequate nutrition, well-drained mediums with moisture retention properties, warmth and light suitable for most plants. The only exception is in dry climates where no-dig gardens will have to be made to suit dry climate species and to allow for less water retention.

Most annuals, perennials, vegetables and fruit trees grow better in Australia than in many other countries because our climate gives enough sunshine and light for growing plants almost all year round. It is important to include some Australian native plants in your garden setting as well as exotic plants.

Some hardy perennials, shrubs and trees such as deciduous fruit trees have deep-rooted and/or widely spreading root systems that require deep, well-drained soils for adequate root growth and plant anchorage. These are best planted into second generation no-dig garden areas: by that time, the soil underneath the garden area will be aerated and rich in humus, and the mulch material compacted and rotted down, providing support for woody plants' root systems. Vegetables with long roots, such as turnips and long-rooted carrots, are also best grown in second or third generation no-dig gardens, provided nitrogen fertilisers are not used when rebuilding the garden. Long-rooted vegetables do not perform as well in first generation gardens as their roots are shortened and often forked.

Many fruits and vegetables can be grown in no-dig gardens. This chapter includes a list of fruits and vegetables and some of their characteristic behaviours in no-dig gardens. Don't be afraid to try growing any plant you want in your no-dig garden.

Planting techniques for no-dig gardens

There are several ways to plant into no-dig gardens. Foremost and the easiest is placing tubers, bulbs, corms, suckers and divisions of perennial root systems straight into the prepared no-dig garden area. Simply make a depression into the top of the garden to plant these, or place them at ground level and build the no-dig garden layers on top of them. Make a knife slit in the base paper layer of the no-dig garden and insert plants under this. Planting is easiest if the material that has been left from first generation or subsequent generation gardens is used, as there is plenty of well-aerated compost-like material to plant into.

Seeds can be sown into the top layer of the garden which, to remind readers, should be well-matured compost, copra peat or a similar material. Seeds can also be pasted onto absorbent strips of paper then planted into the top layer. Another planting method is to create narrow belts of compost on the top of the garden, rather than fully covering the surface, and sow seeds into these. Plants such as tomatoes and potatoes can be planted, with extra layers of no-dig garden material built up around them as they grow.

The space between high gardens can be filled with compost material or substances such as sawdust, and this can be left to rot down for one season. The rotted material is used for topping up the gardens in the following season and for planting into.

Where shallow no-dig gardens are built over persistent weeds, holes can be placed in the paper base and potted plants that have had the pot base removed can be planted so that the top of the pot is at ground level. This protects the plant from invasive weeds and excludes light from any weeds that are there. Plants such as strawberries, blackberries, loganberries, raspberries and some herbs have a suckering habit of growth and thrive in no-dig gardens; they more or less self-replicate without any need for further planting, but they will need thinning for best results.

Plants such as lettuce, feverfew, chives, swede, violets and foxgloves readily self-sow into no-dig gardens but need regular thinning out. When topping up the garden or rebuilding another garden on the same site (see Chapter 5: Ongoing Maintenance), transplant any self-sown seedlings or, as an alternative, place a very thin mulch layer around the plants to prevent stem rot developing on buried plant stems. Take care to control the spread of any weedy species so they don't escape into the surrounding area.

Propagation of plants in no-dig gardens is easy—just stick the cuttings in, or place an extra layer of moist paper over the garden and poke the cuttings through this layer. You may need to protect the cuttings with mini greenhouses or cloches, depending on the type of cutting used.

Companion planting

Companion planting is about selecting plants that will grow well together. There are many important factors that determine this, such as one plant's capacity to attract bees for pollination for its companion plant. Published lists of companion plants are of some help to gardeners but it is a mistake to just use these lists. There are, for example, some plants that have been shown to grow well together in the Northern Hemisphere under vastly different conditions to those in most parts of Australia. It is important to experiment to find which plants do well with other plants in your particular area considering its climate, soil type and rainfall.

In Australia, it has been shown that carrots and potatoes grow really well together, a fact commercial growers exploit. Both plants can grow with limited nitrogen fertiliser and they both require a reasonable amount of water. Too much nitrogen will make carrots grow split multi-rooted root systems. The carrot roots grow below the potato tubers and break the soil, allowing deeper water penetration. The potato foliage provides some shading and wind protection and suppresses weeds. If planting times are judged correctly, the two crops can be harvested at the same time.

It can be surprising which plants will act as companions to others. Bracken fern, usually regarded as a weed, can be grown as a companion for French beans and carrots. The fern provides extra shelter and some wind protection. Its roots go down well into the soil, allowing moisture to accumulate around the root zone when it rains. When bracken rots down, it releases phosphorus into the soil. The shady fronds also offer protection from the hot sun.

Some plants will not grow well together, sometimes because of simple factors such as too much shading. Pumpkins, for example, can overcrowd and shade out smaller plants. Sometimes there is competition in the root zone area (suckering plants) or moisture stress caused by plants that need lots of water (rhubarb). Sometimes it can be simple physical factors such as climbing plants climbing all over others and excluding light. A very small number of plants (walnut trees, for example) seem to give off exudates that prevent other plants from growing near them.

Companion plants do many things. Companion planting can, for instance, provide cross-pollination for fruit trees and bees can be attracted for pollination of vegetables, flowering and fruiting plants, especially tomatoes. Some plants, such as dandelion, can mine deep mineral resources within the soil, which then become available to other plants. Other plants provide support for their companions, for example cornstalks for beans. Some plants provide wind protection; examples here are corn, Jerusalem artichokes, sunflowers and climbing beans on a frame. Others help to retain moisture and provide some weed control by shading the soil (bracken fern, pumpkins, strawberries and many others). Butterflies can be attracted to plants like buddleja and lavender. Such plants as daisies, flowering heads of carrot or parsnip, lovage and plants in the same families can attract and provide food for predator insects. Bird-attracting plants—such as honeysuckle, bottlebrush, banksia and fuchsia—encourage birds to keep insect pests under control.

Plants such as comfrey have deep root systems that mine the soil, resulting in leaves that are rich in nutrients. When the plant dies down, the leaf nutrients are released onto the surface of the garden where worms eat them. Comfrey is also used as a compost additive to speed the composting process and it is a great plant for attracting bees, bumblebees and some birds.

Another plant that can be used in compost is the ordinary stinging nettle. This 'weed' is a good companion for onions. The stinging nettle can also be soaked in water to provide a liquid tea to strengthen plants. Biodynamic gardeners spray a preparation made from the nettle onto plants to enable better use of sunlight by the plants. It also acts as an insect deterrent and the dried leaves have been used as a beneficial mulch and in liquid form as a root drench for tomatoes and other plants.

Most herbs are aromatic and the smell given off sometimes distracts insects from their target plants, preventing insect damage; wormwood and lavender are good examples. Every plant has its own microflora associated with the root zone of the plant and these bacteria, fungi and associated organisms can be beneficial in breaking down plant and animal material and minerals into forms readily taken up by plants. For instance, bacteria associated with legume plants store nitrogen in nodules on the plant roots and when the plant material dies down or is incorporated into the soil, nitrogen is released for other plants. Some gardeners say that the exudates from certain herbs and other aromatic plants actually improve the taste of vegetables growing nearby. Exudates may also help to control some pests and diseases within the soil. Garlic planted around peach trees has been said to prevent peach leaf curl, but this is unsubstantiated. Growing companion plants and practising crop rotation (not growing plants within the same plant family year after year but growing crops from different families on a four-year rotation system) within the vegetable patch helps to prevent the build-up of harmful pests and diseases.

The segregation of the garden into growth zones will help you to organise appropriate companion planting. Plants with ground-hugging foliage, such as creepers (cucumber, for example), and low growth foliage (radishes, as an example) can be placed in a low zone underneath high growth foliage plants (for example, tomatoes or corn) in a high growth zone. Planting in zones allows segregation according to water needs, provides shade for sensitive plants and helps to organise areas for plants that need staking.

Plants suitable for no-dig gardens

Most plants will grow in no-dig gardens, especially one directly on the ground because the soil underneath the garden is improved by successive generation gardens and becomes biologically active and well aerated. In general terms, plants that do well in first generation gardens are those with a shallow but spreading root system, so most vegetables, many cane fruits, and most annuals and perennials are suitable. Any plants, such as carrots, trees, shrubs and deciduous fruit trees, that have long or deep root systems generally need to be planted into second or successive generation garden areas.

Vegetables

All vegetables benefit from no-dig gardens. Shallow-rooted plants such as lettuce, cabbage and cauliflowers will grow an extended root system with a larger percentage of white feeder roots than field or soil grown plants. This makes the vegetables healthier and they will grow larger or crop better. They will also be less stressed and that in turn will make them less susceptible to insect attack and diseases. Even deep-rooted or tuberous plants benefit because no-dig gardens on top of soil create improved soil under the garden to such an extent that the soil becomes very rich with humus, which is loose and friable and ideal for plant roots to penetrate. Tuberous-rooted plants such as potatoes and oca, of course, thrive in these gardens.

To grow as much food in the no-dig vegetable garden as possible, include some fast-maturing vegetables such as radish. Oversowing of lettuce, onions, cress or other plants that can be harvested at an immature stage for salads will provide intermediate crops while slow-growing plants mature. Placing some flowering plants in the garden will attract insect predators and give gardeners some cut flowers. Herbs are always beneficial and useful. Successive plantings of other vegetables can be done to provide a continuous supply of food for the kitchen. Companion planting is something to consider for all gardens but is particularly applicable in the no-dig garden.

Vegetable suitability for no-dig gardens
Artichoke, Jerusalem Best in second generation no-dig gardens because they are subject to wind damage if not well

Growth zones

A planted area can be conceived of as a series of zones depending on the height of the vegetation of the plants in the area. Each of these zones can be considered a growth zone, as shown in the following diagram.

Plants shown left to right: Corn / Climbing beans; Radish or Lettuce; Tomato plant; Lettuce; French bean; Potato; Carrot / Turnip / Parsnip; Onions / Garlic; Pumpkin / Marrow

Underground zone

Zones left to right: Tall zone | Sheltered zone | Reflective warmth zone | Intermediate zone / companion planting zone | Ground cover zone / maximum warmth zone anchored and need staking and root support. Pinching out early shoots makes the plants bushier and less prone to wind damage. Will self-reproduce with tuberous growths. Needs lots of organic fertiliser to perform well. Can be grown in all states.

Broad beans These need rich organic material. Pinch out growing shoots to make them bushier and less susceptible to wind damage. Broad beans grow well in cool climates only and can be grown nearly all year round in cooler areas such as Tasmania. They provide nitrogen to the soil. Will self-seed to some degree.

Broccoli You just can't hold back these plants if plenty of organic manure is incorporated into the garden, but they need regular high nitrogen fertiliser side dressings when the heads start to form. Will grow in all States.

Brussels sprouts Grows well in hay bale no-dig gardens given greenhouse protection but will also grow well in the open. Needs a cool climate to grow successfully and prefers high nitrogen organic fertilisers.

Cabbage Likes the warm root zone provided by composting no-dig gardens and grows exceedingly well. There are many forms. Can be grown in all States and prefers high nitrogen organic fertilisers.

Capsicum Needs warmth and protection in cooler areas and a greenhouse in cold regions but will grow in all States. The use of green grass clippings as a mulch in summer will keep the roots warm.

Carrots There are many forms available. Small-rooted forms are recommended for first generation gardens. Long-rooted carrots are best suited to second generation and successive generation gardens, providing not too much nitrogen has been added. Plant a succession of carrots to provide root crops all year round. Will grow in all States.

Cauliflower Will thrive in rich, organic, layered gardens. Prefers cool-climate areas and needs lots of high nitrogen fertiliser.

Celery Grows exceptionally well because of the plant's need for a constant moisture supply. Can be wrapped in paper, or tubes can be placed over the plants, to blanch the stalks. Will grow in all States.

Chives Best grown as companion plants to other vegetables in no-dig gardens, or used as a border planting. Self-seeds regularly and also spreads by natural division. Will grow in most areas.

Choko Very easily grown from fruits or root cuttings but needs a climbing frame. Try eating the immature fruit for a different taste. Can be grown in all States, even in cooler areas if given protection from frosts and winds. The seed from the choko can be planted out to produce new vines.

Corn Best used in second or third generation no-dig gardens so that the roots can grow into soil underneath. Corn plants do develop aboveground stem roots suitable for extra support, but the plants may need wind protection. Corn is best planted in random thick groups rather than rows. Dwarf sweet corn cultivars are available for smaller gardens. Plant out punnet grown seedlings when they are largish plants; this saves dealing with tiny seedlings and the extra weeding needed. Will grow in all States.

Cucumber Grows just as vigorously as pumpkins and marrows. Can be used as a companion to pumpkins, as an understorey species. Can be grown in all States.

Eggplant Use a grafted one that has a tomato rootstock (or graft your own) for better performance. Can be grown in all States, but may need greenhouse protection in cool areas.

French beans Can be interplanted with other plants that give them a little protection from winds. Beans need a well-drained area. Will grow in all States.

Garlic Best planted into second or successive generation no-dig gardens. Excellent as a companion plant because of its tall, narrow shape. Loves organic matter. Try the huge elephant garlic for a novelty. Grown mainly in temperate to cool-climate areas.

Lettuce Good for any situation, and as companions for tomatoes, herbs and lettuce. Lettuce matures very quickly, especially if grown in mini greenhouses. Use as an interplanted species or grow thickly from seed to provide greens from tiny immature plants. Some old (heritage) varieties self-seed easily and can be used to reseed the garden area. Grows in all States.

Oca Best in second or successive no-dig gardens. Plant into multi-layered, hay bale compost heap no-dig gardens or plant into weed heap no-dig gardens for excellent results. Produces self-replicating tubers, although not until late autumn in cool climates. Not well suited to tropical areas.

Onions For onions, sawdust mulch and blood and bone are good growth media as a top layer of a no-dig garden. Use pre-grown seedlings from punnets to avoid too much weeding. Plant a succession of these to enable early harvesting as greens, and different cultivars for different uses. Grows in all States, but does best in cool- to cold-climate areas.

Peas Often self-seed if pea straw is used in a no-dig garden. Peas prefer a cool climate. They can be used as a cover crop to provide nitrogen for the following vegetable crop. A good companion plant for broad beans and pumpkin. Will grow in all States.

Potatoes Can be multi-layered in large no-dig gardens; they grow well in hay bale gardens, in buckets or in piles of recycled tyres. One of the best performers for no-dig gardens. Grows well in most States, but is susceptible to frost damage in cold areas.

Pumpkins and marrow Excellent for all medium- to large-sized no-dig gardens and do well when planted into compost heap no-dig gardens. Often produce volunteer seedlings in compost heaps. Best placed in a mounded no-dig garden or in a hay bale no-dig garden. Grows in all States.

Radish Fastest vegetable of all, taking only three weeks to produce mature radishes. Often used as a groundcover to prevent weeds on top of no-dig gardens. Radish can be planted as a companion plant with carrots. Requires a temperate climate for best results.

Silver beet Many types available including pink, yellow, orange and red stemmed cultivars. Some plants keep producing for long periods without bolting to seed. Silver beet thrives in no-dig gardens. Plants tend to go to seed when grown in very hot climates but perform well in cooler areas.

Spinach Requires rich organic compost and lots of organic fertilisers. Low growing so can be fitted in with other plants. Grows very well all over Australia.

Tomatoes One of the best. Green grass clippings make a very good mulch for warming roots during cool spring weather. Tomatoes may need staking, but this is optional. They grow well in bales of organic matter and in grow bags. Take care not to water plant stems in hot weather, as this will encourage botrytis stem rot or burning. Do not water foliage. Use mini greenhouses to obtain early tomatoes. Grow basil as a companion plant, but use mini greenhouses on basil to enable its growth to equal the tomato plant. Tomatoes often produce volunteer seedlings in compost heaps. Will grow in all States and all kinds of no-dig gardens.

Zucchini A popular choice for no-dig gardens, producing masses of fruits in mid-season. Try drying thinly sliced pieces to make zucchini chips; they are great. Will grow in all States.

Fruit

Most fruiting trees and shrubs will grow well in no-dig gardens, especially in second or later generation gardens. Fruit trees have strong root systems and prefer a consolidated layer to grow their roots into. However, because some species tend to develop strong downwardly growing root systems to support the plant, the plants may need staking in the initial stages and extra no-dig materials will be needed around the root system as the no-dig garden composts and rots away. If strong-rooted fruit trees, for instance, are planted into the no-dig garden after it has rotted down then this problem may not arise because the soil will have been improved by worm action.

To plant into no-dig gardens, make a hole in the rotted material and plant the tree, heaping the mulch around the root system. Water the roots with a liquid seaweed product. In general, if large woody trees and shrubs are planted in no-dig gardens, it is best to stake them for a while until the roots become established. Any large-growing plants such as citrus trees establish quickly because they have very matted fibrous root systems that spread and stabilise the trees. No-dig gardens actually encourage more fibrous root growth, especially if drenched regularly with a liquid seaweed product. Many feeder roots develop and this helps the tree or shrub to quickly establish in its new environment. The following notes on some fruiting species are given as a guide, but gardeners can consult additional references included in the Bibliography.

Fruit suitability for no-dig gardens

Avocado Seeds of avocado fruit germinate easily in no-dig gardens and can be left to grow to maturity, but it would be best to graft a known variety onto the seedling plant as seedlings may take up to sixteen years before fruiting. Will grow in all States, but in southern areas the plants will need protection from frosts and cold wind.

Babaco Has a spreading fibrous root system and is best suited for second and third generation no-dig gardens. Needs warmth, wind shelter and good drainage, but can be grown in cool areas if wind protection and frost protection are given.

Banana Responds well to no-dig gardens. Suckers well when given food and plenty of mulch material to grow in. Best in tropical or semitropical regions but will grow in southern areas if given a warm, sunny and sheltered position. Grows in all States except Tasmania.

Blueberry Needs acid conditions in growing media. Can be grown in containers. Prefers a temperate to cool climate and grows and produces extremely well in cool-climate areas such as Tasmania.

Elderberry Keep pruned to a bush form for easy control of birds or grow as an espalier! Easily trimmed to shape. Birds feed on the berries if given a chance. Prefers a temperate climate.

Hazelnut Shallow rooted and well adapted for no-dig gardens. Has a fibrous root system ideal for second or third generation no-dig gardens. Will grow in cool to temperate climates.

Passionfruit Has a spreading fibrous root system ideal for no-dig gardens. Use plenty of animal manure to obtain early trellis covering. Suitable for all climates. Many cultivars available; some suited to tropical regions only.

Pawpaw Has a fibrous root system ideal for no-dig gardens. Will grow best in semi-tropical to tropical regions, but the mountain pawpaw will grow in cooler climate areas.

Peanuts Tropical plants, their habit of growth, where the flowers bury themselves in the soil to form the nut, means that a friable, loose medium is needed. Second or successive generation gardens are preferred. They can be grown in home gardens as far south as Melbourne if given protection and shelter.

Pepino This tiny melon is underrated. It prefers long hot summers, warmth and may need greenhouse conditions in cool areas. Several cultivars are available. Will grow in all States.

Tree Tomato Very good plant for no-dig gardens as it has a spreading fibrous root system. Can be grown in pots. Prune every two to three years to ensure the plant's continued vitality. Red, purple and orange fruited cultivars are available. Can be grown in all States, but needs protection in cool areas.

Walnuts and almonds Germinate very well in no-dig gardens. Walnuts can grow into huge trees. Suited to a temperate climate and need cold winters so are best grown in southern Australian regions only.

Watermelon and rock melon Need long hot summer days to mature. Start seedling plants with a mini greenhouse to obtain early growth. Grows best in warm climates with long hot summers.

Herbs

Herbs are excellent performers in the no-dig garden, particularly the self-suckering species such as mints and sage. Herbs act as companion plants for many other plants and provide flowers, perfume and herbal remedies as well as food spices and flavours.

Many herbs, such as the mints, thymes and sages, have creeping habits of growth, underground runner root systems and a suckering habit. Others easily form ground layers, while some have bulbous reproduction systems or seed prolifically. These reproductive systems are enhanced in the no-dig garden: roots grow better, plants send out many more suckers, the plants are a lot healthier and not water stressed so produce more bulbs or offshoots, and healthier plants produce more seed. In fact, no-dig gardens provide such a good environment for herbs that pruning or dividing them to keep them in check will become necessary.

There are too many herbs to mention in this book, but those that grow well in no-dig gardens include basil, thyme, parsley, garlic, mint, lovage, lavender, oregano, nasturtium, savory, rosemary, pyrethrum, marjoram, tansy, wormwood, yarrow, fennel, chamomile, lemon balm, bergamot, borage, chives, dill, dandelion, coriander, foxglove, geraniums and sage.

> ### Making blackberries work for you
>
> An old sprawling blackberry patch can be turned into an organised garden plant that produces ample fruit for home use simply by selective pruning of the old, dead canes and the weaker ones. The idea is to select some of the strong canes of the previous season and mould these into a self-supporting frame. Gardeners can strengthen the canes with the addition of two posts and some parallel wires but if the canes are tied together where they touch, the bush will support itself and this requires no digging at all. The blackberry patch will need to be cut back hard each year and will need regular pruning to make sure it does not become feral again.

Berry fruit

There are many berries suitable for growing in no-dig garden systems. Brambleberries, loganberry, raspberry, lawtonberry, marionberry, thornless blackberry, yostaberry—all of these grow vigorously, many producing suckers that will need to be controlled.

One of the easiest ways to create a no-dig garden of berry fruits is to take winter (or late summer) prunings of blackberry, loganberry or any of the brambleberry vines and just stick or layer them into a pile of raised compost. Many of the running canes are capable of rooting and can be layered into the soil or compost to create new plants; when the tip or stem has rooted, the cane can be cut from the parent plant. You may need to place a trellis, mesh or a couple of posts near the plants to allow them to climb and sprawl, or alternatively they can be allowed to sprawl over the ground.

Strawberries are particularly well adapted to no-dig gardening systems because of their habit of spreading by runners and because they like a lot of organic matter. Strawberry runners usually become available just before winter. They can be planted then or held dormant in the cool part of a refrigerator until needed for late spring or summer planting. Strawberry plants can be poked into hay bale no-dig gardens, and they can be grown in grow bags or containers of any kind including old bathtubs. Strawberry plants produce hanging plants when grown in hanging or elevated containers. The freely hanging plants make harvesting easy, the possibility of pest and disease attack is reduced, and the plants are easy to manage.

Mulching keeps fruit clean. Strawberries can be mulched with a weed-free material such as wheaten straw or dried pine needles, or with plastic sheeting. Strawberry plants are subject to virus infections, spread mainly by sucking insects that inhibit fruit production and cropping. Most strawberries become infected within one to three years, so it is important to obtain new virus-free plants every two to three years to make sure good crops are produced.

Gooseberries love no-dig gardens because of their shallow root systems. They can be grown in containers or trained as an espalier. They need to be pruned only lightly. Use varieties that are resistant to powdery mildew, even though the resistant cultivars available unfortunately lack the taste of some of the hundreds of old heritage varieties. Breeding programs are under way to produce new, tasty gooseberry cultivars resistant to powdery mildew. Refer to the section below on propagation for ways to easily propagate gooseberries.

Black, red and white currant bushes need plenty of organic matter so they are good choices for no-dig gardens. Large piles of fresh grass clippings mixed with a small amount of animal manure and used around plants situated against a hot, north-facing fence will result in good crops even in areas generally unsuitable for currants. Currant bushes perform well in containers providing the roots are kept cool during summer. Surface mulching, painting the pot white or wrapping aluminium foil around the pot (to reflect sunlight) will prevent the roots becoming too hot during the summer months. The container can also be shifted to a position receiving mottled sunlight only. Currants can be espalier trained. In areas where birds are a problem, the plants will need to be netted or the fruit harvested just as it begins to ripen to prevent loss to birds.

Berry fruit are perhaps the most rewarding fruit to grow in no-dig gardens. Even suckering plants such as loganberries and raspberries are more easily managed because sucker growth is so easy to remove compared to suckers growing in heavy soils.

Annuals and perennials

There are thousands of annuals and perennials, most of which grow well in no-dig gardens. There are too many individual plants to deal with all of them here, but gardeners can consult the guides to annuals and perennials (see the Bibliography and Further Reading section) and can be assured that most will do well in no-dig gardens.

Many, such as those used in cottage gardens, self-seed and keep regenerating year after year. Perennials such as foxglove, Californian poppy, ranunculus, cornflowers and aquilegias can all self-seed and intermingle with other plants in the garden. Other perennial bulbous or suckering plants thrive in no-dig gardens and grow extremely well.

Many annuals are purely decorative, grown for cut flowers or used as companion plants (for example, violas and petunias). Many shrubs such as fuchsias will send out low-growing branches that, in well-drained no-dig gardens, self-layer thus helping the plants to spread.

Supplying your own plants for the no-dig garden

All plants for the no-dig garden can be bought from plant nurseries, but this can become expensive. Propagating your own plants is a cost-saving alternative. Some plants, especially heritage plants, are only available as seed through seed savers networks and need to be propagated.

Propagating plants can seem daunting but there are a number of easy ways of propagating, all involving simple techniques and no digging. The approaches described in this section are ideal for people who are not able to spend much time, effort or money on plants, equipment or materials.

Aerial layering is one of the easiest no-dig gardening techniques of propagation for most species of woody plants (for example, fig, lychee, some wattles and rhododendron). Propagation of some of the very hard to propagate plants can be approached this way and with some plants, such as lychees (*Litchi chinensis*), it is the best way to get another plant exactly the same as the parent plant.

Aerial layering is a method of propagating plants above ground level. To start, wound a stem: either slice the stem of the plant at about a 30-degree angle, two-thirds of the way through the stem, and then prop open the cut with a matchstick or plug of mature compost; or alternatively remove a whole section of bark from around the stem of the plant. Once you've done this, cover the exposed area and wrap it in moist mature compost. Then tightly seal this area with plastic sheeting or aluminium foil so as to initiate root formation at the wound site. Leave the plant alone until roots have developed and grown into the mature compost. Then cut the branch (including the roots) from the parent plant at the base and place it in a pot for growing on.

Cuttings taken from plants and stuck into the no-dig garden are particularly successful, especially if planted in second or successive generation gardens, because no-dig garden materials provide a good propagation medium. As described below, the type of cutting or plant piece used for propagation will depend on the type of plant being propagated.

Types of cuttings

Hardwood cuttings Taken from deciduous plants that lose their leaves in winter. The dormant cuttings (30–60cm long) are usually collected during the autumn–winter–early spring period. Suitable for plum (*Prunus* spp.), gooseberry (*Ribes uva-crispa*), fuchsia (*Fuchsia* spp.) and many other plants.

Softwood cuttings Taken from the growing shoots during the plant's growth season, which is usually spring–summer or autumn. Even cuttings from plants such as roses, for example, can be taken provided the cuttings are placed in a container that is fully enclosed with two layers of plastic sheeting over it (the plastic must not touch the cuttings). This creates high humidity and the shoots will not wilt or dry out. Softwood cuttings can be taken from roses (*Rosa* spp. and hybrids), hydrangea (*Hydrangea macrophylla*), chrysanthemum (*Chrysanthemum* spp.) and most other perennial plants.

Semi-hardwood cuttings Taken in summer or at summer's end from the hardening base section of new shoots that are still growing or have just finished active growth. Suited to camellia (*Camellia* spp. and hybrids), rhododendron (*Rhododendron* spp. and hybrids), tea tree (*Leptospermum* spp.) and many others.

Leaf cuttings or sections These can be taken from a few plants such as African violets (*Saintpaulia* spp. and hybrids), camellia (*Camellia* spp. and hybrids), and tuberous begonias (*Begonia tuberhybrida* group).

Semi-hardwood cuttings and softwood cuttings are perhaps the most common types of cuttings. Most Australian plants are propagated from seed, or by semi-hardwood or softwood cuttings. In general, Australian plant seeds germinate well in no-dig gardens and cuttings, once struck, also do well.

For hardwood cuttings, prepare the area for the cuttings by layering paper onto the chosen part of the no-dig garden. Put compost on top of this and then another layer of moist paper. The operation can also be done with just one layer of paper and without the use of compost. Simply push the cuttings through the paper into the soil. Another method is to stick cuttings into the bales of a hay bale no-dig garden in spring; they should develop roots by the end of the summer season.

Semi-hardwood and softwood cuttings are usually 3–10cm in length. Most of the leaves are removed or cut in half. Some gardeners cut the remaining leaves in half to reduce transpiration, but if a very humid environment is supplied (greenhouse or enclosed propagation box) then cutting these leaves will be unnecessary. Stick the lower third of the bare stem of the cutting into the propagation area, with the cuttings very closely spaced, almost touching, for initial rooting to take place.

Leaf cuttings are prepared in several ways. For some plants, such as the African violet, place leaf sections into the no-dig garden with the cut leaf veins in the top layer. Alternatively, just place the leaf stalk into the garden mix or lay the leaf on the surface and place slits with a knife in some of the leaf veins. Spread a thin layer of mature compost on top of the leaf to hold it in place and to encourage plantlet growth.

For all cuttings, use hormone rooting powder, dust, liquid or gel on the base of the cutting before insertion to improve root initiation. The use of rooting hormones is not essential, but with some plants it will make the difference between being able or unable to propagate that species. In general, rooting hormone will produce better rooting and more fibrous roots on cuttings that are treated.

Water cuttings with a liquid seaweed product and they should strike well provided the soil is kept constantly moist to prevent the cuttings from drying out. Plants struck from cuttings can be planted out permanently into the no-dig garden when cuttings have produced a mass of roots. To judge whether a cutting has produced roots, just tug the cutting and if there is resistance this indicates that roots have formed at its base. Cuttings from deciduous plants are best left until autumn or early winter before transplanting.

Some plants simply propagate by themselves. *Sedum rubrotinctum* is one example, but there are many other plants that produce small propagules (sections of plant with roots already forming) including the following:

- aeroplane or spider plant (*Chlorophytum comosum*)
- aloe (*Aloe* spp.)
- kalanchoe (*Kalanchoe* spp.)
- daylily (*Hemerocallis* spp.)
- lilium (*Lilium* spp.)
- piggyback plant (*Tolmiea menziesii*)

The pieces from these plants are simply removed and pushed into a no-dig garden bed.

The spider plant (*Chlorophytum comosum*) and some forms of aloe will form rooted plantlets that hang on the flower stalk section of the plants. These can easily be removed and grown in no-dig gardens. Some kalanchoe plants produce masses of tiny plants along the edge of mature leaves, each one a potentially viable new plant. Many bulbs propagate by forming bulbils or tiny reproduced bulbs. Some of these, such as on liliums, are produced on the flower spike and can be used to supply more plants. Many creepers, for example ivy (*Hedera* spp.), grapevines (*Vitis* spp.) and trumpet creepers or bignonias (*Campsis* spp.), produce adventitious roots (root nodules along aboveground stems), and sections of the stem can be cut off and stuck into no-dig gardens where they will grow into new plants.

Plants such as the large-leafed begonia (*Begonia* hybrids), African violet (*Saintpaulia* spp.), pelargoniums (*Pelargonium* spp. and hybrids), wax flowers (*Hoya* spp.), mother-in-law's tongue (*Sanservieria trifasciata*), and others can grow from leaves or pieces of leaves separated from the parent plants. Simply push the stem of the leaf into the no-dig garden (or lay the whole leaf on the garden) and lightly cover with mature compost. Plantlets will grow from cuts inserted into the leaves (begonia and African violet) or from the base of the stem; these can be cut off and planted directly into no-dig gardens.

Propagation using cut pieces of true bulbs (those bulbs that when cut look like a cut onion) can easily be done with plants such as daffodils (*Narcissus* spp.)

and hyacinth (*Hyacinthus* spp.). All gardeners need to do is cut the bulb into vertical slices; each slice must include a section of the basal part of the bulb (the scarred area where old roots had grown). These slices may be chunky quarter pieces or they may be only 4–5mm wide. The sections contain sliced pieces of unexpanded leaves (scales) and can be used whole or further separated so as to have two fleshy pieces, with each segment containing a small basal part. The segment can be placed into mature compost and allowed to grow new bulbils, which develop between the two fleshy scales. The author successfully tried this system using chunky pieces of daffodil bulbs placed in 100 per cent copra peat.

Another propagation trick with part scales of bulbs or fully formed bulbils is to place them in a small plastic bag with just-moist sphagnum moss, seal the bag and put it away out of sight for a few months. (Plants such as garlic and liliums form bulb scales, which can be broken off separately then used for propagation.) When the bag is eventually opened, young plants will have grown from the pieces or bulbils and these can be transferred to no-dig gardens.

Ground layering is a method of propagating many trees and shrubs that have pliable, arching branches. Select a low branch and make a cut about halfway through the limb. Bend the limb to open the wound and place a piece of matchstick into the cut to keep it open. Peg down the branch to the soil with wire hoops and cover the cut branch section with mature compost. Roots will grow from around the injured area and once this has occurred, the branch (with the roots attached) can be severed from the parent plant and transplanted. Some plants in well-drained no-dig gardens form their own ground layers and all you need to do is cut the rooted pieces from the parent plant and transplant them. Hard-stemmed plants and deciduous plants are well suited to this form of propagation.

Propagating in water All you need to do is put a piece of plant material in a clean jar containing enough clean water to cover the bottom of the cuttings to 5–10cm. Top up the water regularly. Most plant cuttings placed in water will form roots and once roots or root nodules have formed, the cuttings can be transferred to no-dig gardens. Roots formed in a water environment are much softer than roots formed in soil, so take great care when transplanting.

Growing from seed Many commercially available seeds, vegetables in particular, have been presoaked, dusted or treated with chemical fungicides to help with storage and seed preservation. It is important to look at the use-by date on seed packets because many vegetable seeds, such as parsnip, have a very short viability period: after a certain time has expired the seeds will not germinate. Organic gardeners try not to use such treated seed in their gardens, but this is sometimes difficult because a given cultivar may only be available from commercial sources. Seed savers networks (see the Resources section) and some organic seed supply firms do provide

Saving seed

One of the best ways to save seed from soft-fleshed fruits and vegetables such as pumpkin, cucumber and tomato is to collect the seed pulp and spread it on absorbent paper then allow it to dry in the sun. (It is a good practice to first allow the seeds and fruit pulp to ferment in some water for a short while so as to obtain seed that is free of flesh, which may be infected with diseases.) If the seeds are well spread out on the paper, it is easy to cut strips of paper and sow the strip by laying it on the no-dig garden and lightly covering it with compost then watering with a liquid seaweed extract.

To prevent unnecessary waste of seed by overplanting, use an organic paste (such as flour and water paste) to stick the seeds onto strips of absorbent paper. Place the seeds at the planting distances specific to the species and plant the cut strip into the no-dig garden by covering it with a sprinkle of mature compost. This saves time and the seeds stay moist during the initial germination process.

neatly in rows on blotting paper; when dry, cut the paper into strips and plant without removing the seed from the paper. 'Smoking' the seed of some Australian plants with smoke from burning bush grasses and tree leaves will increase the germination rate immensely. Examples of plants that benefit from smoke treatment of seed are lobelia (*Lobelia* spp.), hibbertia (*Hibbertia serica*, *H. lasiopus*), pelargonium (*Pelargonium peltatum*) and lechenaultia (*Lechenaultia floribunda*, *L. formosa*).

Providing warmth for seeds and seedlings

In order to raise your own seedling vegetables, annuals and perennials or to propagate plants using some of the techniques described, it is sometimes helpful to have them inside some kind of protected environment. At times, the top of the refrigerator, the heated area near a gas heater, warm hot water pipes or a warm chimney can be used to warm germinating

untreated seed. Saving seed or joining a seed savers network is an alternative and allows seed swapping.

Sow seed as recommended on the packet, or follow the instructions in any of the vegetable/horticultural handbooks available. Some seeds require special treatment. Scratch the seed coat of hard seeds to allow water into the seed kernel. Place wattle seeds in a heatproof container, pour boiling water over them and leave overnight to soften the seed coat. Seed that is fermented with its fruit in a container and then collected (for example, tomato seed) can be spread

Quick and easy propagation box

A simple propagation box can be made by covering a box or container with an adjustable glass or double-walled plastic lid or top that can be elevated or opened for ventilation. This clear top allows sunlight in, creating warmth that is contained in the box. Shadecloth may have to be placed over the top of the box during hot summer weather to avoid burning of the plants or cuttings. Alternatively, the box can be moved into a shady place.

Rolls of instant lawn are very suited to lawn no-dig gardens.

An alternative lawn—chamomile can be planted as a landscape lawn feature.

A hay bale no-dig garden planted with potatoes and mulched with mulch cubes—a simple but effective way to grow potatoes.

A giant round hay bale no-dig garden hollowed out and filled with compost.

No-dig stacked hay bale gardens growing strawberries.

Tyres, rims and axles were used to make this useful design for no-dig container gardening.

Dutch clogs made into a no-dig hanging garden.

Old farm machinery like this seeder can be made into an attractive no-dig garden display.

A recycled hay mower turned into a garden display.

Paper daisies (*Rhodanthe* spp.) growing in a no-dig hanging garden.

These rotary no-dig gardens at the Kevin Heinze Garden Centre in Melbourne save space and allow easy access.

This no-dig water garden made with plastic sheeting will attract frogs and birds to the garden.

Bathtubs are ideal for no-dig gardening. (The wire grill prevents birds from taking fish or frogs.)

Potatoes perform extremely well in no-dig gardens.

A range of harvested pumpkins grown in a no-dig garden.

seedlings. No-dig gardens can also be built inside greenhouses to take advantage of the regulated warm environment to grow better crops, especially during the cooler part of the year.

Glass-covered greenhouses are the most expensive greenhouses to purchase or make, rigid plastics next and sheet plastic the cheapest. There are, however, many ways to build or create your own greenhouse using recycled materials that will cost next to nothing.

For growing just a few seedlings, small glass-covered units can be purchased or built. One of the smallest types of greenhouse is a propagating box (growing frame) set into the ground and covered with a moveable pane of glass (or recycled window and frame) that can be lifted to allow air circulation or access.

Reuse and recycle

Recycle your PET plastic bottle by using it as a neat little propagation greenhouse. Once the bottle is empty, replace the cap, take a sharp knife and make a slit all the way down one side of the bottle. Force the two sides open so you can place some propagation media along the horizontal base to about 30–40cm thickness. Water the mix using a mist sprayer, then sow seed or plant seedlings into the mix and water again. Close the cut by sealing with glue, sticky tape or some other sealant.

You will have created your own no-dig, mini greenhouse. You won't need to carry out any maintenance or open the bottle for up to five weeks, or until the seeds or seedlings have grown large enough to touch the plastic sides. The bottle can then be unsealed and the plants transferred to the no-dig garden or planted in pots.

To grow plants needing constant warmth, the bottle once sealed can be enclosed in two separate plastic bags, leaving an air gap between the two layers; or, alternatively, bubblewrap can be wrapped around the bottle. This will trap the heat and keep the bottle warm even during periods of freezing cold weather.

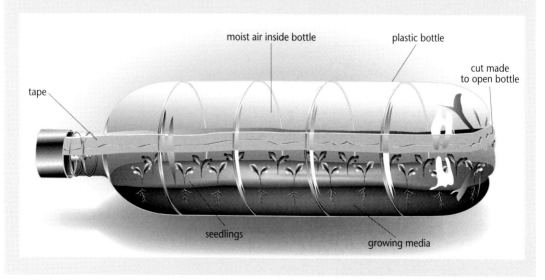

Recycled plastic or glass bottles or containers can also be used to provide warmth.

The cheapest greenhouse can be made from two recycled plastic bags. Plastic supermarket bags are ideal. Take one bag, half fill it with mature compost and place the bag in a cardboard box so the compost will retain its shape. Plant seed, water with a liquid seaweed product, insert wire hoops inside the bag to hold the plastic away from the compost, then tie and seal the bag. Place another plastic bag around the first to fully enclose it and tie this also. The bags can also be used to enclose a pot. The double-walled plastic greenhouse will retain the warmth needed for fast growth of seedlings. Commercially available water-filled plastic tents can also be used to give plants an early start.

The heat given off by composting materials such as grass can be used to provide heat for germinating seedlings. Use a recycled fruit box; drill holes into the base if drainage is needed. Place handfuls of freshly cut grass clippings in the bottom of the box and put mature compost on top of the green grass. Plant seeds directly into the mature compost. The heat given off by the underlying composting grass provides warmth for the seeds to germinate. If glass or plastic sheets are used to cover the top of the box, quick germination is guaranteed. Placing a propagation box on top of an existing warm compost heap will provide extra warmth for unheated boxes.

Mini greenhouses

Hydronurture™ tents (cone-shaped structures made of a series of joined water-filled cells) are excellent for promoting early growth of plants and for encouraging seedlings to germinate and grow faster. They can be used in both warm- and cool-climate areas to advantage. The Hydronurture™ structure can enhance the early fruit production and ripening of tomatoes, cucumbers and rock melons, especially in cool climates, and will boost the growth of most plants during cool weather conditions.

Another form of mini greenhouse can be made by wrapping plastic bubblewrap around three stakes to hold it in place.

If these or similar mini greenhouses are used when planting seeds or seedlings in no-dig gardens, early growth and production and a much better plant survival rate can be expected.

5. Ongoing maintenance

Care and maintenance of no-dig gardens is relatively easy. They have their own stored food within the layers, organic materials within the garden rot down into rich compost that is ideal for root growth and the no-dig garden acts like an absorbent sponge whenever it is watered or rain falls on the garden. In areas that receive regular rainfall, there will hardly be any need to water the gardens.

The garden will need weeding occasionally because wind-blown seed or some seed originating in the layered garden material will germinate and grow. Weeding is very easy, though, as the weeds are growing in loose materials and take very little effort to pull out.

Planting sequences will need to be managed to ensure regular crops and companion planting arrangements will need to be worked out. Regular fertilisation and maintenance of good conditions will prevent animals, pests and diseases from invading the crops. All aspects of maintenance are easily handled with little effort.

One of the most efficient ways to manage no-dig gardens is to use chickens. For those who are allowed by local councils to have chickens on their property, no-dig gardening is simplified. You can build or erect small enclosures for the chickens and allow them to work it over for a period of time until all the weeds and grasses have been scratched up and the earth overturned. The manure from the chickens is deposited on the soil and mixed with the weeds and composting occurs. This breaks down the organic matter and creates an environment ideal for growing plants.

You can make a portable structure of plastic piping and shadecloth or timber and mesh that is easily moved around. The portable chicken house or staked mesh fencing can be moved around in set patterns so that whole areas can be dug up and weeded. Each area is built with a no-dig garden and planted as it becomes available, or clean straw can be placed on the areas to build a potato patch no-dig garden. Contrary to the advice given in most permaculture literature, chickens need to be prevented from moving into areas where vegetables or low plants are growing because, put simply, they eat them or scratch them out.

Topping up and rebuilding

Once a no-dig garden has been used for one year or more, the organic materials within the garden will have rotted down considerably, and in the case of vegetables the first crops will have been harvested. Because some of the material will have rotted down, it will be necessary at this stage to top up the garden with one or two more layers including some fertiliser, or to rebuild the garden entirely thus constructing a second generation garden on the same spot.

Additional fertiliser can be added by applying side-dressings fortnightly or monthly, depending on whether the fertiliser is fast (liquid fertilisers, blood and bone or manure) or slow release (most pelletised or granular fertilisers). Apply side-dressings to the top layer of the no-dig garden, near to but not right against the stem of the plant. Loosely rake the rotted no-dig layer to loosen the material then apply the fertiliser and water it in. Extra layers of organic material can be placed on top if needed. Liquid fertilisers or 'teas' can be given weekly to supplement side-dressings and to enhance the growth rate of plants.

If large trees, shrubs or perennials are planted in the garden, it may not be possible to rebuild the entire garden. In this situation, it is best to place layers around the plants but not directly against the stems or trunks.

Fertilising the no-dig garden

Many types of fertilisers are available to use in no-dig gardens. Following are details of some types of materials that can be used to supply nutrients to the no-dig garden and some of the characteristics that make the materials ideal for specific uses. The emphasis is on organic fertilisers. Water-soluble chemical fertilisers and sprays often kill beneficial bacteria, fungi and other organisms within the soil and can leach into ground water systems. It is far preferable to use organic fertilisers; no-dig gardening lends itself to such approaches. Organic materials used carefully do not have the polluting effects of chemical fertilisers, but it must be mentioned that too much organic fertiliser applied at any one time can also cause pollution problems.

The materials used to build no-dig gardens have already been dealt with in Chapter 2. Many of these provide plant food and build up the soil to create humus. Additional fertilisers that may be beneficial for the garden are dealt with below.

When feeding plants with a liquid food, also use a complementary granular organic fertiliser that allows slow release of nutrients over a long period of time. Foliar applications of one of the many liquid fertilisers available has been found to increase flowering on plants such as fuchsias by up to 70 per cent and is recommended for those plants that respond so well. During the initial stages of growth of young plants, seedlings and transplanted plants, drench the root system with one of the seaweed extracts to promote fibrous root growth and to improve plant health. Foliar applications of liquid seaweed will also help plants to survive drying conditions and rejuvenate transplanted seedlings or shrubs.

Blood and bone and hoof and horn have a relatively high nitrogen content (for organic material) and contain some phosphorus, a few of the trace elements but no potassium. Blood and bone releases its nitrogen very quickly and burning of plants can occur if too much is used, whereas hoof and horn is used as a slow-release fertiliser. Blood and bone is used in conjunction with mulch materials in no-dig gardens and in compost preparation.

Comfrey tea Beneficial fertilising preparations can be made from weeds, stinging nettles and, in particular, comfrey

(*Symphytum asperum* or prickly comfrey). The leaves have a good carbon/nitrogen ratio, rot down quickly and can be added to no-dig garden layers or to compost. Comfrey tea is beneficial and can be made in the same way as seaweed preparations although it matures more quickly, in approximately two weeks.

Fish products are ideal for plant growth and act as a stimulant to the growth of friendly bacteria and fungi within the soil. Liquid fish food emulsions and fish waste mixed with organic matter then composted are available to home gardeners. Fishy liquids, containing nutrients in low quantities, are useful for foliar applications and for drenching the soil.

Organic manures The use of manures in the building of no-dig gardens has already been covered. Manures are best spread evenly throughout all the materials in the no-dig garden. However, most gardeners just layer the manure within the garden structure as they apply each individual material, or place a layer of manure under the newspaper base of a layered no-dig garden. Fresh manures are relatively high in nutrient content but must be used very sparingly, especially when placed close to plant root systems. If the material is well buried in layers within the no-dig garden and a layer of compost or other material used as a topping on the garden, the manure will not burn the roots of plants. This is because the manure will have had time to compost before the plant roots grow down to the manure layer.

Manure teas are the most effective way of applying manure as a fertiliser to no-dig gardens.

> **Manure tea**
>
> Place some manure in old stockings or mesh-like material and steep this in water until a greenish yellow liquid is produced. This prepared liquid can be diluted at 10:1 with water or used undiluted depending on the strength of the manure tea. Seedling plants need the diluted form. Beneficial tea preparations can also be made from weeds, stinging nettles and comfrey.

Composted manures rarely contain much significant food value; the nutrient content of the individual major elements within compost rarely exceeds 10 per cent. This is not enough to feed plants, but gardeners will find that plants such as tomatoes can thrive and produce reasonable crops using a rich compost without any extra fertilisers being applied to the no-dig garden. For best results, though, extra feeding with other products such as rock dust, blood and bone or compost will be required.

Another effective way of using manure as a fertiliser is in pelletised form. Organic manure in dust-like or solid form is easily broken down whereas pelletised material lasts a long time and acts as a slow-release fertiliser gradually releasing nutrients into the surrounding garden. The compressed material has the advantage of being easier to handle, requiring only one-fifth of the space for storage compared to bulk loose manure.

Rock dust (mineral fertilisers) Ground rock particles constitute mineral fertiliser products and are available from several commercial companies. Gardeners can also collect waste dust from rock crushing quarries where the rock being crushed is rich in natural elements (for example, from granite or basalt rocks). All the major plant nutrients can be obtained from raw rock without the rock being chemically treated. Examples are ground rock phosphate (P), ground rock sulphur (S) and ground rock limestone (Ca).

Sprinkle the rock dust onto no-dig gardens as the garden is prepared. Although it may not benefit the first crop grown in that garden because of its slow release of nutrients, the benefit will be noticed in second and successive generation no-dig gardens. Rock dust can result in increased cropping; healthier plants develop when it is used in combination with organic fertilisers and the application of plenty of organic matter. This material should be stored in a very dry place where it will not get wet and set like concrete.

> **Make your own seaweed fertiliser**
>
> Here are step-by-step instructions on how to prepare a homemade liquid or gel from seaweed:
> 1. Collect seaweed, making sure before you do so that you have permission from any relevant authorities.
> 2. Place the seaweed in drums and add enough water to cover the seaweed and a handful of organic fertiliser to help the fermentation/breakdown process. An alternative is to sun-dry the seaweed then break it up into chips that can be diluted with water to make a liquid product.
> 3. Wait until the liquid has turned into a thick, soup-like gel.
> 4. The gel can be used directly on the soil around plants or it can be further diluted with water to use as a foliar spray or as a root drench around plants and seedlings in the no-dig garden.
>
> Dead krill from the seashore may be available in some areas, but permission to collect this must be sought from relevant authorities.

Seaweed products Seaweed is a natural organic plant food. When composted, seaweed is an ideal product to encourage plants to grow and extend their fibrous root systems. Although the nutrients in seaweed are in small quantities, it has been found that almost all the known free elements occur in seaweed including gold. Hormone-like materials in seaweed actually stimulate the root growth of plants. The most useful nutrient sources are the large flat-leafed kelps and the chain-bubble type seaweed. Seaweed products are available in powder, solid or liquid form and can be used as root drenches, mulches or as foliar applications in the no-dig garden. An alternative, if fresh seaweed is available, is to make your own liquid seaweed.

Toilet waste Composting toilets are becoming more popular and the composted waste from these environmentally friendly approaches to human waste disposal can be used as a form of fertiliser. Seek local council advice before using composting toilets or any toilet waste in no-dig gardens.

Urea in its natural form is urine from humans and other animals. This material has been manufactured in slow-release and readily absorbed forms. Most organic gardeners do not use the chemically manufactured form, although it may eventually be accepted by them because structurally it does not differ from the natural product.

Fresh urine needs to be fermented for a while before use because it has a strong smell and is very high in nitrogen. Alternatively, it can be used in a diluted form, with usual rates of dilution being about 10:1. A 10 per cent solution can be applied to seedlings and vegetable crop leaves without burning the foliage or it can be regularly watered into and around the root zone of plants. Some gardeners use the urine directly on the compost heap to supply extra nitrogen.

Worm castings (vermicast) have many times the amount of nutrients in them than the surrounding soil from which the castings were made, so they are a perfect organic fertiliser. The use of worm castings in no-dig gardens has already been covered in Chapter 2.

6. Troubleshooting

No-dig gardening systems are easily managed and require very little maintenance. This chapter covers some of the most common problems associated with no-dig gardening, including non-pathogenic disorders, pests and diseases of plants grown in no-dig gardens and some of the physical/structural facets of no-dig gardening and approaches to dealing with them.

Physical problems

There are a few physical problems particular to no-dig gardens. The most common problems are discussed below, together with solutions to them.

Aeration Deep and multi-layered no-dig gardens can suffer from a lack of aeration because the layers compress leading to a lack of air, particularly in the centre. Hip-level no-dig gardens allow for easy access but they can easily become waterlogged (see also Waterlogging below). Sometimes plants such as tubers will not grow in the centre of the garden because of lack of air. One solution is to place plastic aeration pipes (5–10cm in diameter) through the centre of the garden. To be suitable for aeration, tubular pipes must have holes drilled about every 8cm, preferably in a spiral, all along them. Place these pipes about a metre apart through the garden for best results. Gardens of half a metre or less in depth should not need extra aeration.

Drying This occurs when layers have been inadequately watered (see Watering below) and may also occur when materials compost rapidly and the resultant heat dries the bed. Drying can happen in shallow or deeply layered gardens. Monitoring of the condition of the no-dig garden layers will allow timely watering if needed.

Fire hazard if dry If no-dig gardens are allowed to dry out, they can become a fire hazard. This is really only a problem when poor management allows the garden to become completely dry or when poorly stacked hay bales spontaneously combust.

Nitrogen draw-down When no-dig gardens are built without adequate nitrogen (in the form of fertilisers or highly nitrogenous materials), plants in the garden may show a distinctive yellowing and lack of growth. This is called the 'nitrogen draw-down effect' and occurs because the composting process within the garden is using all the available nitrogen and leaving none for the plants. To fix the problem, apply liquid nitrogen to the foliage and roots of the plants and place organic manure around each plant within the garden.

Runaway weeds/plants Some plant species—such as the weed sorrel, couch grass and clover—tend to invade no-dig gardens and have to be carefully controlled in their initial stages of growth to prevent them from becoming established. If they do become established, the roots will form an almost impenetrable root mat layer in the garden. Then the only way to remove them is to chip the matting and roll it up like a carpet.

Slippery mulch Sometimes a layer of paper or other material can become slippery during wet periods. Extra mulch on these areas will soak up excess moisture and prevent accidents from happening.

Slugs and snails These pests can become a problem in moist straw or hay that creates a sheltered environment (see the following section called 'Pests and diseases in no-dig gardens').

Stability of edging Small no-dig gardens generally need edging in order for them to maintain their shape and not collapse. Recycled timber, bricks, concrete blocks, railway sleepers and hay bales make excellent edging and can be added if the garden shows signs of collapse.

Sunken middle If the centre of an edged no-dig garden has been filled with loose instead of compressed material, the centre of the garden, as it composts, may sink lower than the outer edges. Where this is likely to happen, it may pay to grow tomatoes or potatoes in the centre of the first generation garden, as these plants respond to having extra material built up around them, which can be done as the garden sinks. An alternative is to grow a succession of quick-maturing crops such as radish and top up the area with extra compost before planting the next crop. Another alternative is to put springy materials such as prunings at the centre of the garden to give support to the middle of the no-dig garden.

Watering Esther Deans suggests that no watering of separate layers is needed for shallow no-dig gardens. Although watering will not be needed where there is regular rainfall, in very dry areas some watering will be required. Deeply layered gardens that use dry or water-repellant material such as pressed dry wheat straw will need to be watered as each layer is built, otherwise a dry area may develop at the centre.

Waterlogging No-dig gardens require only infrequent watering. Even in extremely dry weather conditions, the garden will survive without regular water applications. Because of this, during long periods of wet weather, the garden can become waterlogged. Extra drainage will help to prevent this or, when extreme wet weather threatens, a cover or tarpaulin can be put over the garden to redirect some of the rainfall. No-dig gardens in bathtubs or other containers may become waterlogged if the drainage point is blocked. Often, the extra weight of water in a bathtub-type garden (see Chapter 3: Types of No-Dig Gardens) will press the plughole outlet into the soil and prevent adequate drainage. Check the drainage outlets regularly, especially after heavy rain; or provide rock fill around the outlet.

Pests and diseases in no-dig gardens

No-dig gardens, like any other gardens, can be attacked by a range of pests and diseases or be affected by some non-pathogenic disorders. Mulches in no-dig gardens cause some particular problems and these are dealt with first. This section

Common pests and diseases of no-dig gardens

General	Vegetables	Fruit trees	Trees and shrubs
Ants	Aphids	Apple and pear scab	Leaf miner
Armillaria	Blossom end rot of tomatoes	Bacterial gummosis	Mealy bug
Botrytis		Birds	Mites
Damping off	Cabbage moths	Brown rot	Rose black spot
Grasshoppers	Carrot weevil	Citrus gall	Stem borer
Loopers	Celery leaf spot	Codling moth	
Mice	Chocolate spot on broad beans	Light brown apple moth	
Scale			
Slime mould*	Cockchafer grubs	Peach leaf curl	
Slugs	Early and late blight	Pear and cherry slug	
Snails	Eelworms	Penicillium rot	
Toadstools*	Heliothus caterpillar	Silver leaf	
Weeds	Parrots	Sooty mould	
	Rhubarb leaf spot	Vine black spot	
	Sparrows	Vine downy mildew	
	White fly	Vine moth	

*These are in fact not pests but beneficial organisms you might find in a no-dig garden.

also outlines a selection of the common problems as they affect vegetables, fruit trees and other trees and shrubs. All the pests and diseases covered are summarised in the above table.

Further help with pests and diseases can be found in the Resources section.

General problems

Because no-dig gardens are based on materials composting, a few organisms may be encountered. Some are beneficial while others can cause problems. The most common are dealt with below.

Ants can be a particular problem for no-dig gardens because they can colonise compost heaps or thick layers of organic matter in no-dig gardens. In general, they do no harm (there are exceptions, such as Argentine ants and other pest species) and can in fact be beneficial because they eat/store weed seeds and eat grubs and bugs that are in the garden.

Ant colonies in no-dig gardens generally occur in a dry pocket of the material. Aerating the layer by vigorously poking a rod through the garden and watering thoroughly will get rid of ant colonies because ants do not like wet conditions. Ants such as the jack jumper and the bull ant have a nasty sting and can be hazardous. Liquid pyrethrum sprays can be sprayed directly onto ants or can be poured down holes into the nest to destroy whole colonies.

There is a common misbelief that ants spread scale. Some species do appear to spread scale and then use the scale as a food source, however, the spread of scale is probably caused by the tiny mite-like juvenile scale accidentally crawling onto the legs of ants and dropping off at another site. Ants gently squeeze both aphids and scale insects, causing them to exude a sticky highly nutritious substance on which they feed.

Armillaria Armillaria is present in most Australian States and Territories and can be introduced to no-dig gardens via infected materials. Untreated material such as wood and bark chips from trees may be infected. Armillaria is a fungal disease that infects native eucalypts and is spread slowly through wet soils by spore-like growths. The fungus has a distinct fruiting part, a honey-coloured mushroom with white gills and white spores. Very few plants are resistant to this disease once it is established. To get rid of infection, the soil has to be sterilised, removed or sieved to remove every piece of stem or roots of the infected plant. Plants that have shown some resistance include: Abelia (*Abelia* x *grandiflora*), mock orange (*Choisya ternata*), Japanese spindle tree (*Euonymus japonicus*), myrtle (*Myrtus communis*) and double-flowered spiraea (*Spiraea prunifolia* 'Plena').

Botrytis This is a fungal disease present in most environments. The spores (seeds of the fungus) are carried about in the air. It shows as a fluffy, grey mould-like growth on infected tissue, usually at ground level and particularly in damp, enclosed environments where there is little air movement. It can attack most plant seedlings, cuttings used for propagation and mature soft tissue annuals and perennials. Botrytis can be a particular problem with no-dig gardens during prolonged wet weather periods.

Ensuring adequate air movement between plants, seedlings or cuttings will help to prevent infection. Using well-aerated dry mulch such as straw under strawberry fruits will reduce infection, as will removal of all the old plant material for hot composting at the end of the season (see Chapter 2). Crop rotation in vegetable beds will help, as will keeping no-dig materials away from the stems of tiny, immature seedling transplants. Plant stems should not be watered during very hot conditions as this may burn or injure the stem and provide an entry point for the disease.

Damping off This disease is most commonly observed when seedlings grown in open soil or in punnets or trays suddenly fall over. Examination of the lower stem will reveal a softened, discoloured area that has rotted and weakened the stem at soil level causing the stem to bend. Several bacteria and fungi can cause damping off but they are usually phytopthera or fusarium fungal species. To treat, dispose of any infected soil or soil mix, and wash and sterilise pots before re-use. Damping off organisms can attack any germinating seed or seedlings. For prevention, don't plant seeds too thickly, don't overwater, and make sure there is plenty of air movement around seedlings. Avoid watering from overhead, if possible. Use a well-aerated seedling mix conforming to Australian Standards.

Grasshoppers, especially in the nymph stage when they have no wings, can be devastating to any plant and will strip all foliage from them. The only real protection is the use of netting. However, neem, an extract from the neem tree (*Azadirachta indica*), shows good results as this product acts as an anti-feeding agent and insects starve to death (see the Resources section).

Loopers are caterpillars with long bodies. They have gripping legs at both ends and not in the centre of the body and so 'walk' by pulling the back section up to the front, forming a loop as they do so. The body is also looped when the creature is at rest. These interesting larvae rarely occur in large numbers and can be removed by hand.

Mice These small rodents tend to live where there is shelter and food available and can invade layered no-dig gardens. They will use as food such things as developing potato tubers on potato plants. Live-in mice can be deterred by aerating the no-dig garden layers and making sure the whole garden is moist.

Scale An incredible number of species of scale insects attack a large number of plant species that grow in no-dig gardens. Some have a waxy covering while others are woolly or have a hard shell. Mature insects are usually oval-shaped domes that can be seen sticking to the plant. The immature scale moves around and looks like a mite. It is the mite stage and the egg stage that can be controlled with one or more sprays of light oil or soapy water. Chilli extract sprays can also be effective.

Slime mould grows at a phenomenal rate and can appear in the no-dig garden almost overnight as a coloured frothing spreading mass of goo. There are various forms that are coloured brown, yellow, orange or purplish. The organism causing this is related to fungi and bacteria. Slime mould is actually good for garden plants as it breaks down organic matter and provides nitrogen to the no-dig garden.

Slugs These are perennial pests, as no-dig gardening is all about gardening using materials that slugs love to breed in. Slugs can devour young or just planted seedlings or emerging seedlings seemingly overnight. They leave a typical bitten edge to leaves that have some see-through sections at the edges where veins are showing. The leaf is only eaten on one side. Slugs also leave visible slime tracks.

In dry areas, where it is possible to keep the immediate area around the plants free of moisture, slugs will not be

---

Drunken slugs!

To make a beer trap, take a saucer-shaped container with slippery sides and pour stale beer in it to attract slugs. Place the container with the lip at soil level near the plants to be protected. Another simple idea is to use plastic funnels with the stem end blocked with a piece of cork.

so much of a problem. Attracting native Australian birds and building up the biological activity within the garden will help to control pests including slugs. Companion planting of an outside border of lettuce, a plant that slugs love, can protect the main crop. Keeping chooks, geese or ducks to control slugs and snails is only a good idea if you intend to replant the whole area where the birds are let loose, as they also love vegetables and don't discriminate between slugs and cabbage leaves.

Two safe organic remedies are beer traps and collection. Collection of slugs is best done with a torch at night when the slugs are on the move.

Homemade dust baits can also be used. Although the slug and snail baits on the market are not registered as organic by organic organisations, products containing an iron compound, or metaldehyde, are reasonably safe as they break down to non-poisonous by-products.

Snails can be collected more easily than slugs. The best time is a rainy night. Thrushes and other birds eat snails and should be encouraged into the garden area with bird-attracting plants and food sources. However, some birds (for example, wrens and sparrows) also love small lettuce leaves and these plants may need to be protected with netting, especially at the seedling stage. Snails can be killed using the same methods as used for slugs (see above), but they can also be encouraged to shelter in a dark, moist place above ground level.

Crushed shells, diatomite and sharp sand and lime are supposed to deter snails, but once wet these materials are not effective so they can only be used in dry areas, sheltered no-dig gardens or in greenhouses.

Toadstools No-dig gardens use layers of organic matter as the basic structure and fungi are often the prime organisms breaking down and 'composting' the material. They have fruiting bodies in the form of mushrooms or toadstools and can often be seen in the no-dig garden. These fungi are beneficial and do no harm.

Weeds Traditional no-dig gardens will have very few weeds, especially if a non-weedy layer such as well-composted material or copra peat is placed on top of the garden to plant into. Weedy materials can be used within the layered no-dig garden, provided this layer is covered up by other non-weedy materials. Some weeds will grow from seeds blown in, but these are easily pulled out. Wetted newspaper as a mulch on top and around the plants in the no-dig garden will help to suppress any weed growth.

Snail trap

How many times have you shifted old bricks or damp blocks of wood and found snails underneath? Using this knowledge you can build an effective trap for snails. Build a shelter with bricks or wood blocks then cover this with wet bagging or old carpet to keep the area moist. Check every day for snails.

Pests and diseases of the vegetable garden

If vegetable crops are grown organically with plenty of nutrition and water, crop rotation and weed control, common vegetable pests and diseases are less likely to attack. The most common pests and diseases are described below, together with organic control measures.

Aphids These tiny, mostly flying insects cluster on new stems or on sappy sections of a large range of vegetables, annuals, perennials, shrubs and trees. They exude a sticky, sappy substance that can attract black sooty mould, a fungus that lives on the exudate. Aphids have soft bodies and can be destroyed by a strong jet of water. Soapy water will also cover their breathing holes and suffocate them. Organic sprays such as pyrethrum, light oil sprays and chilli extract will also kill aphids. Commercial sprays containing mixes of garlic extract, pyrethrum, chilli extract, soap, vegetable or mineral oils are effective against most pests including aphids.

Blossom end rot of tomatoes is common on tomatoes in no-dig gardens and is caused mainly by calcium deficiency, although other factors such as soil and air temperature, available nutrients and lack of water can contribute to its formation. It creates a blackened end to the fruit. To prevent blossom end rot, make sure the plants have plenty of food, give them a side-dressing of lime (or incorporate lime into the no-dig garden) and water frequently so that the plants do not wilt or become stressed.

Cabbage moth/butterfly There are two major insects that attack brassicas (for example, cabbage, cauliflower, broccoli, Brussels sprouts): the white cabbage butterfly and the diamondback moth. The white cabbage butterfly is very common in no-dig gardens and is quite easy to see. The diamondback moth is tiny (less than 10mm long), hides in plant foliage and is rarely seen unless disturbed. Both lay their eggs on plants, and these hatch into voracious green caterpillars. The larvae of the white cabbage butterfly chew whole sections of leaves. The diamondback moth larvae, on the other hand, often eat a layer on one side of the leaf surface and the damaged area will turn whitish and give leaves a freckled or flecked look. This is often the first indication that the moth is about. *Bacillus thuringiensis*, an organism that attacks larvae, is particularly effective against white cabbage moth and is available in a dust form. Other cabbage dusts are also effective.

Carrot weevil Carrot weevil larvae nibble small chunks out of carrot roots, especially those left in the garden for an extended period. A short harvest time will help to control them. Crop rotation is also important. If carrots are grown in the same spot year after year, carrot weevil will increase dramatically. Encouraging biological activity in the no-dig garden will also help.

Celery leaf spot Celery is a bog plant that needs constant moisture. If it suffers moisture stress, it becomes susceptible to this disease, which shows as irregular spots and blotches on the leaves, causing the leaf edges to curl and eventually die. The organically recommended copper spray Bordeaux will control its spread, but infected plants should be pulled out and burnt or hot composted (see Chapter 2) to get rid of the reservoir of infective spores.

Chocolate spot on broad beans Healthy plants rarely get this disease. Chocolate spot shows as dark brown spots all over the leaves of infected plants. Overhead watering will spread the disease from one plant to another. Bordeaux sprays will help to control it but if only one plant is infected, pull it out and destroy it before nearby plants succumb to the disease. Chocolate spot is sometimes mistaken for rust, but bean rust produces hundreds of small pustules over the top of the leaf surface with the underside of the leaves showing tiny yellowish spots. Rust is controlled organically by using powdered sulphur dust. Regular applications of potash are also said to help control chocolate spot.

Cockchafer grubs are often called curl grubs because the white grubs, larvae of small beetles, are usually curled into a 'C' shape when dug from the soil. They feed mostly on pasture grasses but when an area is freshly cleared for gardening, they have no readily available food and will attack young plant seedlings or nibble their root systems. Indications of attack are seedlings found fallen over and chewed off at the base. The best way of avoiding attack is to leave any newly cleared area vacant for several months before planting to enable the grubs to relocate. Chooks can be let into newly cleared areas for a few days to clean out all insects and grubs.

Early and late blight Tomato leaves are subject to early and late fungal blights, which start as a damaged area on the leaf that may appear watermarked. The area then turns black or brown. The diseases, caused by different organisms, are spread by overhead watering, so it is best to just water the base of the plants. Remove any leaves that show initial infection and spray or dust with a copper or sulphur fungicide such as Bordeaux and powdered rock sulphur (dust only). Any plants that have all their leaves infected should be removed and destroyed. Staking the plants will also help to improve aeration and increase airflow.

Eelworms are very tiny; indeed most cannot be seen with the naked eye. They live on the roots and leaves of plants. Some species are parasitic on insects and are used as a means of biological control. Common eelworms (nematodes) cause problems with many host plants including vegetables such as tomatoes and potatoes. The plants become weak, often stunted, and the roots or tubers of the plants develop knotty protrusions that look like warts. Diseased plants should be culled, and the affected tubers of potatoes should not be replanted. Once established, eelworms are very hard to eradicate. Fallowing (leaving unplanted) the infected area for two to three years and practising judicious weed control can help. Strict crop rotation, including the use of grain crop plants such as wheat and oats that are not eelworm hosts, will help to control them.

All kinds of vegetables, like this selection of heritage produce shown by Michael Fanton of Seed Savers Network, will thrive in a no-dig garden.

Companion planting in an aboveground no-dig garden.

Raspberries are just one of the many berries very suited to no-dig gardening.

A weedy blackberry trained into a useful espalier.

A punnet of freshly picked stawberries from a no-dig garden.

Aloe (top) and Kalanchoe (above) species produce sections of plant with roots already forming and these can be used for propagation.

Stem and leaves of *Sedum rubrotinctum*, a plant that is easily propagated in no-dig gardens.

An African violet leaf showing new plants arising from the leaf surface.

Daffodil bulb pieces (quarters) propagated in a no-dig garden tray in a greenhouse.

Gooseberry plants form their own ground layers and these can be used to produce new plants.

Propagating in water is a simple way of creating new plants for the no-dig garden.

Mac Boyd of Donald, Victoria, demonstrating an easy to make an inexpensive propagating box with plastic covering.

Paper impregnated with spaced seed for direct sowing—an excellent idea for no-dig gardens.

Double layers of plastic fitted over a propagating box to act as a mini greenhouse.

Heliothus caterpillar These caterpillars of moths from the *Noctuidae* family are usually about 40mm long and occur in several different colours: dark brown, light brown, black–green, green or yellowish with dark- or light-coloured stripes along the side. They are also called budworms because of their habit of attacking flower buds, developing seeds and ears of corn. They can attack the leaves and the heart of plants such as lettuce, eat leaves of potatoes or burrow into tomatoes. In other words, they have a very diverse plant host range. Check vegetables regularly and destroy any grubs you find. Catching infections early reduces the likelihood of further build-up. Organic dusts and *Bacillus thuringiensis* in dust form can be helpful.

Parrots, particularly the green rosella, can be a problem in no-dig gardens. The birds are adept at digging up potatoes. Signs of parrot damage are small peelings of potatoes near garden beds. Make sure that potatoes are well mounded over with no-dig garden material to prevent easy access. Parrots can also damage flowers and buds of fruit trees and other trees and shrubs and these may need to be completely netted over.

Rhubarb leaf spot Because of its poisonous leaves, rhubarb rarely gets attacked by insects; however, it is susceptible to leaf spot especially if it is water stressed. The infection point on the leaf darkens then becomes dead and dries to a rusty red colour. Serious infections will see whole leaves develop a mottled reddish pattern. Remove the first leaves infected and spray the plant with Bordeaux.

Sparrows Peas just about to be picked are often attacked by sparrows and other birds that bite through the pods to eat the seeds. Netting the plants completely is the only effective protection.

White fly is a common insect that invades many plants. In the vegetable garden it is mainly seen on tomatoes and French bean leaves. The insect is shaped like a tiny white moth. Its nymph stage, while so tiny it can only be seen with a magnifying glass, does the damage by sucking the sap from plants. Organic sprays of pyrethrum or chilli extract, or organic dusts, will give some control. However, the best method of control is to hang yellow-coloured cardboard in and around the plants to attract the flies. Smear a thick see-through grease or glue onto the cardboard to trap the flying adult insects. Mineral oil applications can help to kill the nymph stages by suffocating them. Parasitic wasps are also available from some companies dealing in biological control supplies (see the Resources section for details).

Pests and diseases of fruit trees

Following is a list of the most common pests and diseases affecting fruit trees, with organic control methods for each.

Apple and pear scab Apple scab can be controlled by regularly spraying with a water and lime solution—one small handful of lime to 10 litres of water. The solution must be stirred constantly while spraying to prevent the lime from settling. Some gardeners prefer to stir the material thoroughly, let it settle and then only use the lime wash water as a spray. If the solution is too strong, it will kill leaves so be careful with the amounts used and do not spray during very hot conditions. Sprays of lime sulphur or Bordeaux in winter will also help to kill dormant spores.

Bacterial gummosis mainly affects stone fruits such as cherry, apricot, almond and peach. It shows as bleeding sap globules on limbs or twigs and may cause whole limbs to wilt and die during extended hot weather. Remove and destroy infected limbs and paint Bordeaux on cut limbs. Sterilise cutting tools with methylated spirits or bleach before using them to cut other branches. Copper sprays with Bordeaux in autumn, winter and early spring can help, and summer pruning instead of traditional winter pruning is recommended.

Birds are a perennial problem in gardens, vegetable areas and orchards. The only truly effective way to prevent too much damage is to use netting to protect the affected plants.

Brown rot This fungal disease infects blossom, small shoots and fruits of stone fruit trees, particularly apricots, and can severely reduce crops. Removal of all dead fruit, dead twigs and all visible sap on the tree during winter is advisable, and spraying with Bordeaux at pink bud stage is recommended. If a tree becomes infected, remove the dead and dying parts immediately to prevent further spread, even if this means pruning while the tree is in bud or has leaves and fruits already developed. Summer pruning instead of winter pruning is also recommended. The tree must be pruned so that the foliage is opened up to allow plenty of wind and air movement through the tree.

Citrus gall causes swelling of twigs and limbs on citrus trees and can severely distort the growth parts. The galls are caused by a tiny wasp laying eggs in soft young shoots. The eggs hatch into tiny grubs whose feeding creates a reaction in the tree which results in swelling of the tissue. The only effective control is to cut and remove all swollen parts from the tree (in late spring or summer) and burn the pieces. This may mean cutting the citrus tree virtually to a stump but it is, nevertheless, the only way to control the problem. Watch for signs of reinfection and remove infected twigs immediately.

Codling moth can be controlled to a considerable degree by using pheromone traps, sticky traps, cardboard wraps, wine jars (jars filled with wine), collecting fallen fruit, and practising companion planting (see the Further Reading section for sources of more information).

Light brown apple moth is a native Australian insect that has a huge host range. It belongs to the leaf roller group of moths whose larvae curl the plant leaves and bind them with webbing to create a shelter in which to live. The larvae are slightly more than 10mm long, thin, and light, bright green. When disturbed they are very active. They forage and eat leaves and the skin of fruit such as pears but rarely become a real problem. They can be controlled with *Bacillus thuringiensis* in dust form. Keeping the garden weed free will also help as the larvae live on many weed species such as fat hen (*Amaranthus* spp.). Collecting and squashing of curled leaves will control larvae numbers considerably.

Peach leaf curl infects nectarines and peaches and causes distorted and enlarged leaves and can blemish fruitlets with a bubbling reddish scarring. The disease is caused by a fungus that attacks the tree at bud swell stage; to control, spray with Bordeaux at this stage. Bud swell is when the buds are just starting to swell, not when buds are already swollen. Most gardeners are too late with their spray and consequently have little success in controlling the disease.

Pear and cherry slug gets its name from its appearance: it looks like a small, black, slimy, slug about 10mm long. It is actually a grub with small stumpy legs underneath the body, but seems to rely on the slime it produces to move along on leaves. It eats leaves to the point that only skeletons remain. It is important to catch the early infections. Dusting the leaves with powdery substances like talcum powder, dirt dust or wood ash can act as a control and *Bacillus thuringiensis* in dust form may also work. Sprays containing hot chilli extract are also worth trying. In very hot weather the larvae seem to perish without spraying.

Penicillium rot Many rots invade citrus fruit and one of them is penicillium, which causes a blue mould to develop. Sprays with Bordeaux during spring or late summer are recommended to control most citrus fruit rots. Lightly pruning the base of the tree and the internal foliage area to allow air movement through the tree will dramatically reduce the incidence of these diseases.

Silver leaf is a fungal disease that infects most deciduous fruiting trees and some ornamentals. It gets into the tissue of the plant and can cause death of limbs, twigs and spurs. Sometimes the plant may show few symptoms except that the leaves have a silvery appearance. The only form of control is to remove the infected branches from well below the infection point. It is important to sterilise cutting equipment before pruning a branch that is not infected, or before pruning any other trees or shrubs, as the disease can be spread in the sap that is deposited on cutting tools.

Sooty mould is a black sooty material that accumulates on the leaves and stems or trunks or fruits of many plants. It is actually a fungus living on exudates of insects such as aphids or scale. If the insect populations are controlled then the sooty mould will disappear. On hardy shrubs and trees such as citrus, a spray of half-strength Bordeaux will wash off the sooty mould quickly.

Vine black spot is a fungal disease that causes black patches to grow on the canes and leaves of grapevines. The main control procedure is to remove all infected parts of the vine during the winter pruning operation and then spray the plants with Bordeaux. Follow-up sprays with Bordeaux can also be applied.

Vine downy mildew is a disease occurring during warm weather that infects the leaves and fruit of grapevines. On leaves it first shows as oily spots that cause the tissue to turn yellowish; the infected area eventually dries out and becomes brown. Fruit often have a furry growth on them or may turn a grey colour and become very hard. Spraying with copper and sulphur sprays controls the disease and Bordeaux sprayed in winter will help to kill any dormant spores.

Vine moth The common vine moth lays eggs that hatch to black spiky grubs with yellow, red and white markings. These grow to about 4–5cm in length and can devour leaves at a prodigious rate. *Bacillus thuringiensis* in dust form will kill these larvae easily. Small infestations can be controlled by collecting and destroying the grubs.

Pests and diseases of other shrubs and trees

Shrubs and trees grown in no-dig gardens can be attacked by many of the same insects and diseases previously dealt with. The following common problems can also affect fruit trees and other plants in the no-dig garden.

Leaf miner These are insect larvae from several varied insects including beetles, moths, wasps and flies. The larvae may attack several species of plant or be specific to only one. Many annuals such as nasturtiums are attacked, as are some vegetables such as cauliflowers and citrus trees. The characteristic damage is scribbly markings on leaves caused by larvae tunnelling inside the leaf structure. The tunnel area becomes pale and bleaches white, so that trails of the feeding larvae are easy to see. Because the larvae are inside the leaf, only systemic insecticides will be able to kill them. Usually, though, the damage occurs on only a few leaves or during certain seasons and this small amount of damage is probably acceptable in an organic garden. If the first leaves invaded are picked off and destroyed, further spread may be prevented. The citrus leaf miner can be controlled by applications of a fine light oil spray.

Mealy bug is a slow-moving, oval-shaped insect covered in grey–white woolly material that is water resistant. It usually has two tailpieces sticking out like antennae. It attacks many plants, including indoor potted plants. Mealy bug is very hard to get rid of because it has the ability to hide in crevices and cracks or in between developing leaves. Pruning the affected part from the plant can be a method of control; destroying the whole plant is the other option. Some gardeners daub cotton wool soaked in kerosene or methylated spirits on the insects to kill them.

Mites are so tiny you cannot see them with the naked eye. They are not true insects: under a microscope they look like small spiders. They hatch from tiny, almost see-through, eggs. Heavily infested plants will show minute leaf speckling. Severe populations will create webbing that can be seen all over the plants. Organic controls are sulphur dust and micronised chilli extract sprays. Predator mites that kill pest mite species are also available for home gardeners (see the Resources section for details).

Rose black spot This is a very common disease in plants that have not been selected for disease resistance. Some newly available cultivars show some resistance. Infected leaves will show black spots, often surrounded by a yellow edge. Organic control measures include a spray made up of mineral or vegetable oil mixed with liquid seaweed at the recommended rate of dilution. Winter applications of Bordeaux will help to control latent spores on and around the plants.

Stem borers are the larval (grub) stage of several species of insect. They attack plant stems by burrowing under the bark layer and ringbarking the branch, causing it to die. Many plants are affected by stem borer. The only sure control measure is to cut out the grub, jab wire into the hole to kill it, or remove the affected branch.

7. Educational and community no-dig gardens

Many people today lack understanding of basic agriculture and horticulture and knowledge of plants and soil life. This is partially because of lack of training and because of the concentration by schools and other educational institutions on theoretical, rather than practical, material together with the lack of importance associated with gardening and horticulture in general. The widespread use of computers has also exacerbated the problem. There are exceptions to this and some schools are trying to introduce practical garden projects for children.

In their everyday lives, children are bombarded with glossy advertisements for takeaway foods that offer only limited nutritional value. These products are often loaded with salt and sugar. Current storage and marketing methods ensure that people have reduced opportunities to buy or taste really fresh produce at its best and may grow up with little appreciation of how things grow or how to grow things themselves. Working parents under pressure of time and commitment often have no time to garden or are living in houses, units or flats that only have a very tiny gardening space.

One of the easily managed, less time-consuming ways of getting young people involved with plants is to give them the opportunity to build no-dig gardens and to have them plant their own vegetables, annuals or perennials in these gardens. No-dig gardening projects for schools reduce the need for management and upkeep by staff and mean that children can learn about nature, the interaction of birds, bees and insects and other animals, the biology of plants and the science of soil. They have the chance to grow and produce their very own food that is full of nutrition and tastes marvellous. They can learn about seed germination and plant growth. The gardens can also be used to grow annuals, perennials, trees and shrubs. Children will have a worthwhile activity and be able to show their resourcefulness. No-dig gardens can be built from recycled products; they can be individual, portable or done as a class project. A worm farm can be established as part of the project to provide worm castings and nutrients for the garden.

No-dig gardens can be built very quickly and planted on the same day. For young children especially, this is a major advantage as they can see the results of their labours and can get to the interesting part of planting without having to go through the long and sometimes tedious process of digging and preparing conventional garden beds. Maintenance tasks on no-dig gardens are minimised because no-dig gardens absorb and hold water, meaning they do not have to be watered as often. Very few weeds invade these gardens so weeding, often a boring and time-consuming task especially for children, is minimal. There are lots of simple ways to make gardening enjoyable for children, as this chapter will show.

No-dig gardens can be built to any shape or size and be placed anywhere. Demonstrations of no-dig gardening can teach people about recycling, nutrition and organic gardening, and give them an interest in plants. This approach has application to wider community involvement in horticulture and agriculture. Community gardening, also dealt with in this chapter, is another way in which the principles of no-dig gardening can be put to good use.

No-dig gardening for children

Many of the types of gardens already dealt with in Chapter 3 are readily adaptable for children, but there are lots of ways children can be encouraged to grow their own food. The simplest vegetable for children to grow is the bean shoot.

Children can easily build other gardens in pots. Lots of secondhand things can be used as fun pots for plants: half wine barrels, old washing machine tubs, heritage wash troughs, plastic drums, metal drums, milk cartons and crates, and recycled polystyrene fruit boxes. Rubbish bins or compost bins can be made into instant potted gardens and old clothing can be employed to make fascinating potted or hanging forms. Try using socks to make caterpillars, or old hats for a hanging basket. Worn out shoes and boots make great plant pots and can be painted whatever colours suit.

A recycled, cleaned plastic bottle, jar or flagon can be used to create a mini greenhouse for growing plants and seedlings and the structure also protects the plants from such pests as rabbits, birds, snails and slugs. Cut out or remove the base of a large jar, bottle or flagon and use the remaining part as a cover for young seedlings, just planted seeds or small plants. A recycled plastic bottle can also be used as a self-contained greenhouse.

The above mini greenhouse can be used to propagate plants from cuttings or children with 'green fingers' can just push cuttings into the soil then cover these with a homemade plastic tent made from supermarket bags, making sure that sticks or wire keep the plastic from being in direct contact with the cuttings.

Grow your own bean shoots

An ordinary glass (or plastic) jam jar can be used to grow all sorts of shoots for salad greens. The most popular are bean shoots, alfalfa, cress and onion.

Put the seeds in the jar and place a fine mesh material over the top as a lid. This can be a piece of an old stocking gathered around the lid and held in place with a sturdy rubber band. Soak the seeds for a couple of hours or overnight then turn the jar upside down and drain to encourage germination. Lay the jar on its side near a window in a warm room. Once or twice a day, depending on the weather, add water to the jar to wet the seeds and developing sprouts then immediately drain them and return the jar to the sunny spot.

When the shoots are long enough (usually when they completely fill the jar or container), they can be harvested for salads and garnish.

A portable mini bag garden

Using a bagful of copra peat, peat moss or soil mix, children can create a portable mini garden in a bag. Simply poke holes for drainage in one side of the bag and slits on the other side for planting cuttings, annuals, perennials or vegetables or bulbs. To aid watering, partially insert a plastic funnel into the top of the bag. Pour in nutrient solution at regular intervals to supply moisture to the plants. In cool areas, two wire hoops can be placed over the bag and anchored in the soil and one or more clear plastic sheets used to create a plastic igloo to keep the plants warm.

Recycling old clothing hardly seems to be associated with gardening, but old socks can provide plenty of garden fun. Filling socks with your recycled kitchen waste—after it has turned into compost—and planting seed or plants into the prepared no-dig sock will give you an instant garden. All you need is some old socks.

Another obvious way to utilise old clothing and to have fun with gardening is for children to make their own scarecrows. The clothing can be stuffed with straw, tying it together and squeezing shapes into heads, arms and legs. The 'Hairy Harry' idea could be used to make the head of the scarecrow, so that the scarecrow ends up with a head of living grass. The scarecrow can be a useful addition to the garden, frightening birds away from the vegetable or fruit garden areas. Once the scarecrow has deteriorated with use, it can be used as a no-dig garden or as a material layer within a no-dig garden.

Scarecrow competitions are a fun way to spend a day or weekend. Scarecrow competitions are becoming increasingly popular and are held at fairs, field days, shows and at places such as Rippon Lea National Trust gardens in Melbourne.

A simple hydroponic garden

Instructions, adapted from *Tomatoes for Everyone*:

1. Use a small pot with drainage holes in it.
2. Fill with a good soil mix, copra peat or peat moss.
3. Place or squeeze the pot inside another see-through, non-draining pot or container (e.g. a plastic soft drink bottle with the top half cut off) leaving an air gap at the base of the inside pot.
4. Plant a tomato plant, vegetables or flowering plant such as petunia in the inside container and water with a seaweed product.
5. Add water and allow the water to come up the base of the inside pot. (A string wick can be placed between the water and the tomato seedling: push it through the drainage holes at the base of the pot or insert it at soil level at the top of the pot, making sure one end of the wick is in the water so it will draw water into the pot. However, this is not essential.)
6. Keep an eye on the pot and fill with water every time the water level gets low.
7. Pelletised slow-release organic fertilisers can be placed on the surface of the soil mix in the pot.
8. Foliar sprays or manure teas can be applied to the leaves for extra nutrients if needed. Apply nutrients at the beginning of the day to allow the leaf surface time to dry before nightfall.

A simple hydroponic garden in a bucket.

Competitions could be extended to include all types of 'Hairy Harry' creations: animals, birds or people could be made from recycled socks and put on display.

A simple method of no-dig garden that children (and adults) can try for starters is a 'spud in a bucket'.

One excellent pastime for children of all ages is to create their own imaginary spud friend. This is how it is done: select the biggest, ugliest lumpy potato you can find. Use your imagination to create a head and face of the potato. Paint lines, eyes, mouth and face on the potato using a waterproof coloured pen. At the place where the top of the head is situated, cut off the top. Make a hollow about 2–3cm deep in the top of the head where it is cut, then place some potting mix or compost in the hole. Obtain some grass seed and plant them into the top of the head, then water with liquid seaweed. Within a few weeks the potato friend will have developed living green 'hair' on its head. The grass 'hair' will continue to grow and can be regularly cut and styled. Seeds other than lawn seed that can be

An easy greenhouse

1. Using a knife and secateurs, cut along one side of a plastic bottle.
2. Force the bottle half open.
3. Lay the bottle on its side and put seedling mix into the bottom of it.
4. Moisten the mix with a misting spray of water or liquid seaweed extract.
5. Place the seeds or seedlings in the mix.
6. Water with a liquid seaweed product.
7. Close up the bottle, sealing it with masking tape or glue.
8. Place the mini greenhouse in a spot where it will receive full sun.
9. Extra warmth will be retained inside the propagation area if the whole bottle is enclosed in a sealed plastic bag or wrapped with sheets of bubble plastic.
10. Leave the container alone for two to four weeks until the seedlings appear. Some shading may be needed for seedlings to prevent sunburn during very hot weather.
11. Open up the bottle and transplant the seedlings or plants into the open garden or into pots.

This is a quick and easy method, ideal for children to try because it requires no maintenance between sowing and transplanting.

Hairy Harry

Make an imaginary plant creature. Paint a face on a sock or stocking or sew buttons on it to resemble a face. Place a thin layer of seed inside the sock on the side or area that will be uppermost when the creature is finished. Carefully fill the rest of the sock with compost or a soil mix. (An alternative to sowing the seed on the inside of the sock is to pat them firmly onto the outside of the formed shape in the desired location. Mix flour and water together over a low heat to make a glue then paste it onto the sock.)

Tie or seal the sock, making sure to pack the mix in tightly to form the desired shape. Shapes could also be stitched into the sock so that when the sock is filled with growth medium, the material pushes out into the shape required. The shapes are up to the imagination of the gardener—mushrooms, caterpillars, grubs, aliens and human-like heads can be formed with great success.

Water the sock and after a while the seed placed in the sock will germinate to create a living art form, for instance a face with growing green hair (Hairy Harry). The growing 'hair' can be trimmed to create a different hairstyle each month and the cut grass can be recycled back into the compost bin.

Water the garden regularly or place the end or underneath side of the sock in a container to which water and nutrients have been added or drip fed.

Seeds commonly used for no-dig sock gardens are lawn grasses; annuals such as petunias, begonias, viola, herbs, salvia, marjoram, parsley, thyme; and vegetables such as onions, garlic chives, lettuce and radish. Some of the herb seeds used for green shoot harvesting could also be planted in the sock to create green shoots of alfalfa, cress or mustard onions which can be cut for use in salads or as a garnish.

Hairy Harry.

used include annuals such as petunias (*Petunia* hybrids), violets and violas (*Viola* spp.), strawflowers and daisies (*Rhodanthe* and *Bellis* spp.). Creeping plants that hang down such as black-eyed Susan (*Thunbergia alata*) and climbing fig (*Ficus pumila*) are especially good. Mondo grass (*Ophiopogon japonicus*) or rat's tail cactus (*Aporocactus flagelliformis*) will give different hair-do effects.

Children can also create their own styled apple gnome from fallen apples in the garden. The apple is cut and carved to the shape of a gnome's head or any other shape. The cut flesh can be drenched or squirted with lemon juice to delay browning, and the apple placed in an airy dry spot and allowed to dry naturally. The head will change shape and develop

Spud in a bucket

Choose a bucket. Punch drainage holes in its base. Select a good healthy potato (preferably a seed potato to guarantee it is disease and virus free) and place this in a bucket. Collect some compost and cover the potato. When the potato plant starts to grow, allow the foliage to grow out of the bucket, then cover the lower stems with rich compost. The bucket can be gradually filled provided about 20–25cm of foliage remains uncovered. The potatoes can be harvested any time the gardener wishes. Immature small potatoes taste magnificent, so there is no need to delay harvest until the whole plant dies down.

Scarecrow.

crinkles and new faces as it ages and dries. When the face has fully dried, it can be decorated—a hat can be made for it, and it can even be used as the head of a doll or small scarecrow.

Two types of plants are really no-dig gardens in their own right and some children might enjoy learning about these plants and looking after them. These are staghorn ferns (*Platycerium superbum*) and some orchids. These plants can be tied to rocks or tree trunks. The only requirement of the gardener is to fix the plants firmly onto the supporting tree or structure with wire, straps, nails or mesh. Staghorns and elkhorns can easily be attached to fences, tree stumps or around the base of living trees to supply lovely weeping fronds of foliage. Orchids such as rock orchids (*Dendrobium speciosum*) (in temperate regions and the tropics) can be

Illusion gardens

Illusion gardens or gardens of time can be created in a small, insignificant, unused part of the garden to create a landscape feature that gives depth and a feeling of space. These gardens can be built in very small spaces (for example, on balconies, or in tiny patio or garden spaces) or even against a wall. They are geometrically constructed so as to give an illusion of receding space. Illusion gardens are fantastic features to add to a limited gardening space. They can be no-dig gardens: all you need is potted plants, tiles/ceramic materials, bricks and maybe some lattice work to create an imaginary garden. Children can have a lot of fun making their own illusion gardens while learning about the effects of receding space.

placed into rock crevices or on trees and some of the cymbidium orchids (*Cymbidium* spp.) will also survive this treatment in temperate zones.

Community gardens

Many local council authorities in collaboration with community groups develop gardening areas for use by the general public. These are developed on council or unused ground and are set up for the benefit of those people who want to garden but may not have the space to do so. Many people living in flats, units or retirement villages do not have access to a garden and enjoy community gardens.

Air plants and hanging gardens

There are some fantastic plants that can be used to create no-dig air gardens. All that is needed is to lift the plants into place, attach or glue them to a support and leave them there. Some bromeliads can be stuck with glue upon glass, plastic, wooden frames, or any material to act as wall hanging plantscapes that will exist with minimum maintenance. The bromeliad Spanish moss (*Tillandsia usneoides*) is also called the air plant because it can live in air. In its natural habitat, it just clings to tree branches as a support, getting all its needs from converting sunlight into food. This plant needs no maintenance at all.

There are many other varied plants in the Bromeliaceae family. Most of them rely upon trapping water in their tubular leaf/stem structure as a method of sustenance, so that they require very little maintenance. In cool areas bromeliad plants are often hung in the shade of trees or wired into place to obtain partial sunlight. In the tropics these plants can be grown in the open.

Some plants produce living plantlets attached to the mother plant or germinate seed while still attached to the mother plants. These tiny plants, called propagules, can easily be removed and placed into pots, requiring no digging at all. The best examples of the self-propagating plants are some of the agaves (*Agave* spp.), which produce underground suckers, as well as the following:
- the aeroplane or spider plant (*Chlorophytum comosum*), which produces aerial plantlets
- the chandelier plant (*Kalanchoe tubiflora*), which produces plantlets at end of leaves
- daylilies (*Hemerocallis* spp.), which produces plantlets on the flower spikes
- strawberries (*Fragaria* spp.), which produces runners
- currant bushes (*Ribes* spp.), which has self-layering branches
- tiger lily (*Lilium* spp.), which has bulbils on the flower stem

Some of the creeping plants with rooted or self-layered stems—such as ivy (*Hedera* spp.), pineapple-scented sage (*Salvia elegans*), mints (*Mentha* spp.) and viola (*Viola* spp.)—can easily be transferred and grown in pots, something children might enjoy learning to do. Simply snip off pieces of plant that contain the roots and place them in a no-dig garden, hanging baskets, pots or containers. If self-watering pots are used, the upkeep/maintenance will be minimal.

There are many, many ways in which children and young people can be fired with enthusiasm for gardening. No-dig approaches are simple and easy as well as being fun.

Simple propagation using a plastic bottle as a mini greenhouse.

Each garden within the site is rented out at low rates and gardeners can use the plots to grow whatever they want to. Community gardens allow people to meet new friends and get some exercise.

Community garden areas are one of the best places to develop no-dig gardens. The site need not have excellent soil types or drainage; it could be a reclaimed area, a disused block or an area normally full of weedy growth. No-dig gardens can actually improve the soil and its drainage and will add commercial value to the site.

Council mulched waste from prunings and all grass cuttings could be layered over large areas. Organic fertiliser could be added and the whole area planted to a crop such as potatoes. This single crop would help to break up the soil and aid in weed control. After the initial cropping, the area could be divided up into separate plots; important for access and so that people can take responsibility for smaller areas. Organic gardening principles could be adopted thus giving individuals and communities access to clean food.

No-dig gardens are easily prepared without too much organisation or preliminary work being needed, are a low cost initiative, and are easily managed. Recycled waste material can be used to build the gardens, and the produce can be consumed by the local community growers or given to charity or schools. Functions can be held at the community garden centre, and competitions and educational field days can be organised.

The Knox community garden in Melbourne is one such site. This was the area chosen for trialling a giant no-dig display garden; the circular garden when finished was 9m wide. It had about 25cm of chipped mulch layered over newspaper and a thin layer of lucerne straw. Interspersed through the mulch was a trailer load of chicken manure. At the centre of the garden, a wire mesh circular 'hub' 2m high and 3m wide was erected. This mesh cage was used to grow climbing plants against and for building a compost pile. The nutrients leached from the compost spread outwards to the garden area, providing nutrients for the growing vegetables. The garden was left to compost for several weeks before planting began. All crops tried in the garden did very well, particularly lettuce, cucumber, potatoes, radish and tomatoes.

The Knox garden is one of a growing number of community gardens established or in the process of being established in urban areas and in a few country towns throughout Australia. Interest seems to be growing, and as more and more people are starting to enjoy active retirement while living in small spaces without gardens, the idea of community gardening becomes very attractive. People with no area in which to garden can also find community gardening an outlet for their interest in plants and people. Living in a community and using community gardening as a social event is a way of life for many gardeners. No-dig gardening is a practical way to make community gardening easier, as well as being a way of encouraging more people to become interested in gardening and use it as a path to better understanding of the food we eat.

An example of a commercial propagation unit.

Hydronurture™ igloo double-walled cells filled with water—great for fast growth of seedlings.

Portable chicken runs make life even easier for no-dig gardeners.

The no-dig garden on the right is well supported by timber sides; the unsupported one on the left, however, is starting to slump.

Waterlogged strawberries in a bathtub no-dig garden—the cause is a blocked outlet.

Tomato seedlings showing damping off symptoms. Damping off commonly affects seedlings grown in punnets for use in no-dig gardens.

Eelworm (nematode) damage on potato tubers. Once established, eelworms are very difficult to eradicate.

Potato scab can be caused by over-liming of soils.

Heliothus grub on Penstemon flowers.

Immature plum fruits attacked by aphids.

Sooty mould on grapefruit.

Codling moth larvae in developing pear fruit.

Leaf miner in nasturtium leaves.

Wax scale on the stem of a pittosporum species.

Two-spotted mites and webbing on a Cape gooseberry plant.

Resources

Peak organic industry body in Australia

Organic Federation Australia
452 Lygon St, East Brunswick VIC 3057
tel: (03) 9386 6600, fax: (03) 9384 1322
website: www.ofa.org.au
email: info@ofa.org.au

Certification bodies

Australian Quarantine Inspection Service (AQIS), GPO Box 858, Canberra ACT 2601; tel: (02) 6272 3933, Freecall: 1800 020 504, website: www.aqis.gov.au
email: organic@aqis.gov.au

Biodynamic Research Institute, Main Rd, Powelltown VIC 3797
tel:/fax: (03) 5966 7333

Biological Farmers of Australia (BFA),
PO Box 3404, Toowoomba Village Fair,
Level 1, 456 Ruthven St,
Toowoomba QLD 4350
tel: (07) 4639 3299, fax: (07) 4639 3755,
website: http://www.bfa.com.au
email: info@bfa.com.au

Eco-organics of Australia,
PO Box 198, Coraki NSW 2471
tel: (02) 6625 1500, fax: (02) 6683 2815

National Association for Sustainable Agriculture Australia (NASAA),
PO Box 768, Stirling SA 5152
tel: (08) 8370 8455, fax: (08) 8370 8381
website: http://www.nasaa.com.au
email: enquiries@nasaa.com.au

Organic Food Chain,
PO Box 2390, Toowoomba QLD 4350
tel: (07) 4637 2600, fax: (07) 4696 7689

Organic Herb Growers of Australia Inc.,
PO Box 6171, South Lismore NSW 2480
tel: (02) 6629 1057
website: www.organicherbs.org
email: president@organicherbs.org

Organic Vignerons Association Australia,
PO Box 503, Nuriootpa SA 5355
tel: (08) 8562 2122, fax: (08) 8562 3034

Other useful organisations

Australian Community Gardens Network,
PO Box 446, Kogarah NSW 2217
tel/fax: (02) 9588 6931
website: www.magna.com.au/~pacedge
email: pacedge@magna.com.au

Australian Garden History Society, Royal
Botanic Gardens, Birdwood Ave,
Melbourne VIC 3141
tel: (03) 9650 5043, fax: (03) 9650 8470
Freecall: 1800 678 446
email: aghs@vicnet.net.au

Australian National Botanic Gardens,
GPO Box 1777, Canberra ACT 2601
tel: (02) 6250 9450
website: www.anbg.gov.au/anbg

Australian Tree Seed Centre, CSIRO
Forestry and Forest Products,
PO Box E4008, Kingston ACT 2604
tel: (02) 6281 8211, fax: (02) 6281 8266
website:
www.ffp.csiro.au/tigr/atscmain/index
email: atsc@ffp.csiro.au

AWGA Vermiculture Inc. (formerly
Australian Worm Growers Association),
Secretary, PO Box 30, Merriwa NSW 2329
Publicity Officer tel: (02) 4920 1188
website:
www.dragnet.com.au/~lindah/awga/AWGA

Bio-Dynamic Farming and Gardening
Association Australia Inc.,
PO Box 54, Bellingen NSW 2454
tel: (02) 6655 0566, fax: (02) 6655 0565
website: http://www.biodynamics.net.au

CERES (Centre for Education and
Research in Environmental Strategies),
8–10 Lee St, East Brunswick VIC 3057
tel: (03) 9387 2609, fax: (03) 9381 1844
website: www.ceres.org.au
email: ceres@ceres.org.au

Collingwood Children's Farm,
PO Box 80, Abbotsford VIC 3067
tel/fax: (03) 9417 5806

Garden Clubs of Australia,
PO Box 237, Thirroul NSW 2515
email: membership@gardenclubs.org.au

Henry Doubleday Research Association,
Secretary, 816 Comleroy Rd,
Kurrajong NSW 2758
tel: (02) 4576 1220
website: www. hdra.asn.au
email: hdra@hdra.asn.au

Holmgren Design Services,
16 Fourteenth St, Hepburn VIC 3461
tel: (03) 5348 3636
website:
www.spacountry.net.au/holmgren/
email: holmgren@netconnect.com.au

Kevin Heinze Garden Centre,
39 Wetherby Rd, Doncaster VIC 3108
tel: (03) 9848 3695

Nursery and Garden Industry Australia,
PO Box 907, Epping NSW 1710
tel: (02) 9876 5200, fax: 9876 6360
website: www.NGIA.com.au

Permaculture International,
PO Box 6039, South Lismore NSW 2480
website:
www.nor.com.au/environment/perma
email: permed@nor.com.au
pacedge@magna.com.au

Permaculture Research Institute,
c/o PO Box, The Channon NSW 2480
tel: (02) 6688 6222, fax: 6688 6499
website: www.permaculture.org.au
email: pri@permaculture.org.au

SEED (Sustainability, Education and
Ecological Design) International,
50 Crystal Waters, Kilcoy Lane,
Conondale QLD 4552
tel/fax: (07) 5494 4833
website: www.permaculture.au.com
email: info@permaculture.au.com

Soil Association of South Australia Inc.,
PO Box 2497, Adelaide SA 5000
tel: (08) 8277 5385

SSN (Seed Savers Network),
PO Box 975, Byron Bay NSW 2481
tel: (02) 6685 7560, fax: (02) 6685 6624
website: www.seedsavers.net
email: info@seedsavers.net

The Food Forest,
PO Box 859, Gawler SA 5118
tel:/fax: (08) 8522 6450
website:
www.users.bigpond.com/brookman
email: brookman@bigpond.com

WWOOF (Willing Workers on Organic
Farms), W Tree via Buchan VIC 3885
tel: (03) 5155 0218
website: www.wwoof.com.au
email: wwoof@wwoof.com.au

Useful publications

Acres Australia
Freepost 1, PO Box 27, Eumundi QLD 4562; tel: (07) 5449 1881, fax: (07) 5449 1889, Toll free: 1800 801 467
website: www.acresaustralia.com.au
email: editor@acresaustralia

Australian Horticulture
Rural Press Magazines, PO Box 254, Moonee Ponds VIC 3039
tel: (03) 9287 0900, fax: (03) 9370 5622
email: subscriptions.net.circ@ruralpress.com

Burke's Backyard
PO Box 929, Willoughby NSW 2068
website: www.burkesbackyard.com.au

Earth Garden
PO Box 2, Trentham VIC 3458
fax: (03) 5424 1743
website: www.earthgarden.com.au
email: info@earthgarden.com.au

Gardening Australia
GPO Box 9994, Hobart TAS 7001
tel: 1300 656 933
website: www.abc.net.au
email: gardening@your.abc.net.au

Grass Roots
Night Owl Publications, PO Box 242, Euroa VIC 3666
tel: (03) 5794 7285

Green Connections
PO Box 793, Castlemaine VIC 3450
tel: (03) 5470 5040, fax: (03) 5470 6947
website: www.greenconnections.com.au
email: green@castlemain.net.au

Greenhouse Living
Grass Roots Publishing Pty Ltd, PO Box 117, Seymour VIC 3661
tel: (03) 5792 4000, fax: (03) 5792 4222

Greenworld
Glenvale Publications, PO Box 347, Glen Waverly VIC 3150
tel: (03) 9544 2233, fax: (03) 9543 1150

The Organic Gardener
PO Box 1067, Lismore NSW 2480
tel: 1300 656 933
email: hummingwords@ozemail.com.au

Useful websites

Backyard Organic Gardening:
www.backyardorganicgardening.com

GardensOnLine:
www.gardensonline.com.au

Gardenweb: www.au.gardenweb.com

Global garden: www.global-garden.com.au

Horticulture Australia:
www.horticulture.com.au

Organic Gardening from Down Under:
www.organicdownunder.com

Seed suppliers

There are many suppliers of seed so this list should be seen as a starting point only.

Bay Seed Garden (organic seeds)
PO Box 1164; Busselton WA 6280
tel: (08) 9752 2513, fax: (08) 9752 1399

Diggers Seeds
105 La Trobe Pde, Dromana VIC 3936
tel: (03) 5987 1877, fax: (03) 5981 4298
website: www.diggers.com.au
email: orders@diggers.com.au

Eden Seeds
MS 316, Gympie QLD 4560
tel: (07) 5486 5230, fax: (07) 5486 5586
Freecall: 1800 188 199

Fairbanks Selected Seeds
542 Footscray Rd, Melbourne VIC 3011
tel: (03) 9689 4500

Goodman Seeds
PO Box 91, Bairnsdale VIC 3875
tel: (03) 5152 4024 or (03) 5152 1262

Green Harvest
52 Crystal Waters, MS 16,
via Maleny QLD 4552
tel: (07) 5494 4676, fax: (07) 5494 4674
Freecall: 1800 681 014
email: greenhar@ozemail.com.au

Green Patch Organic Seeds
PO Box 1285, Taree NSW 2430
tel: (02) 6551 4240

Hendersons Seeds
165 Templestowe Rd
Lower Templestowe VIC 3107
tel: (03) 9850 2266, fax: (03) 9850 6794

Henry Doubleday Research Association
Secretary, 816 Comleroy Rd
Kurrajong NSW 2758
tel: (02) 4576 1220
website: www.hdra.asn.au
email: hdra@hdra.asn.au

Mr Fothergills Seeds Pty Ltd
22 Prime Drive, Seven Hills NSW 2147
tel: (02) 9838 0500

New Gippsland Seeds and Bulbs
PO Box 1, Silvan VIC 3795
tel: (03) 9737 9560, fax: (03) 9737 9292
website:
www.possumpages.com.au/newgipps/index
email: newgipps@bigpond.com

Phoenix Seeds
PO Box 207, Snug TAS 7044
tel: (03) 6267 9663, fax: (03) 6267 9592
email: phnx@ozemail.com.au

SSN (Seed Savers Network)
PO Box 975, Byron Bay NSW 2481
tel: (02) 6685 7560, fax: (02) 6685 6624
website: www.seedsavers.net
email: info@seedsavers.net

Yates Seeds, Arthur Yates & Co.
PO Box 4072, Milperra NSW 2214
tel: 1800 224 428
website: www.yates.com.au

Organic control products and techniques

Many materials and methods are used to control pests and diseases organically in the garden. The ones listed below are a guide only.

Aeration Prune plants to allow airflow through them and prevent the build-up of diseases

Bacillus thuringiensis in dust form A biological bacteria that attacks larvae (grubs) of several insect species, including cabbage white butterfly

Baking soda Often used in diluted form to control diseases

Basal watering Watering around the base of plants instead of on stem or foliage to prevent fungal and bacterial diseases

Beer traps Stale beer attracts slugs and snails

Bordeaux A mixture of copper sulphate and lime that mainly controls bacterial diseases

Copper tape Has been used around plants to stop slugs and snails from attacking plants

Crop rotation Planting different plant family groups in individual garden plots each year for four years in a crop rotation system to avoid the build-up of pests and diseases specific to one plant family group

Derris dust A dust from plant material that controls several insect problems

Eelworms Used to control some soil borne insect larvae

Enviromat™ mulch collars Can be placed around plants for weed control

Fruit fly traps Traps to attract and kill fruit fly adults and prevent them from breeding

Hydronurture™ igloo A water-filled, cellular-ribbed igloo that can be used to protect plants and to give extra warmth, which boosts plant growth especially during cool weather conditions

Insect predators (mites, wasps and eelworms that eat pest species are included in this group): can be purchased and released to control various specific problems in the garden

Jiffy Pots™ Compressed peat moss plugs suitable for seed germination and propagation

Lime dust/powder Used for making Bordeaux; and when mixed with water has been used to control apple scab disease; the dust puffed on leaves will also control pear and cherry slug

Lime sulphur A corrosive liquid used as a fungicide that will control some bacterial and fungal diseases

Liquid seaweed Various brands available, the product is used as a soil drench and foliar spray, and provides minute quantities of nutrients for plants and seems to help with pest and disease resistance build-up in some plants

Maxicrop™ See Liquid seaweed above

Milk Used as a spray on leaves to control some powdery mildew infections

Mineral oil Used to control insects and kill insect and mite eggs

Multiguard Slug and Snail Pellets™ Contain an iron compound that breaks down into harmless organic products and is non-polluting

Natrakelp™ See Liquid seaweed above

Neem A plant extract that kills insects by making them virtually starve to death

Netting Used to prevent bird and animal predation

Orange oil (citrus oils) Used to control some insects and their eggs

Paper bags Placed over fruits before they are ripe to prevent fruit fly, birds and other attacks from insects such as European wasps

Pestoil™ An oil product useful for controlling many insects such as scale, citrus leaf minor and aphids

Pheromone traps Use to attract male codling moth insects and prevent them from breeding

Pruning Opening up the bush or tree to allow air movement will reduce the build-up of diseases

Pyrethrum A broad spectrum spray that will kill all insects; use with care, read the label

Pyrethrum, garlic and capsicum spray Useful for controlling most insects

Quassia chips Steeped in boiling water then the extract is used on plants to discourage possums

Seasol™ See Liquid seaweed above

Soapy water Smothers insects and scale

Sticky traps Glue on the trap surface holds and traps insects such as white fly

Tea tree oil Used as an antiseptic, cleansing agent and for control of some diseases

Vitec Fish Food Emulsion™ A fertiliser used as a foliar spray or liquid root drench that seems to build up disease resistance in some plants

Wasps Predatory wasps are used to control pests such as scale and codling moth larvae

Bibliography

Adams, G., 1989, *Birdscaping Your Garden*, Weldon Publishing, Sydney, Australia.

Anthony, D., 1997, *The Ornamental Vegetable Garden*, University of New South Wales Press, Sydney.

Ashworth, S., 1991, *Seed to Seed*, Seed Saver Publications, Iowa, USA.

Australasian Biological Control, 1995, *The Good Bug Book*, Australasian Biological Control Inc., et al.

Australian Broadcasting Corporation, 1999, *Australia's Open Garden Scheme Guidebook*, ABC Books, Sydney.

Baker, K. F., 1957, *The UC System for Producing Container Grown Plants*, University of California, USA.

Ballinger, R. & Swaan, H., 1982, *Vegetable Gardening in South-Eastern Australia*, Caxton Press, New Zealand.

Bartholomew, M., 1981, *Square Foot Gardening*, Rhodale Press, Emmaus, Pennsylvania, USA.

Beazley, M., 1997, *The Complete Book of Plant Propagation*, Reed International Books Ltd, London.

Blazey, C., 1994, *The Diggers Club Guide to Gardening Success*, Doubleday, Australia.

Blombery, A. M. & Maloney, B., 1998, *Growing Orchids in Australia*, Kangaroo Press, East Roseville, NSW.

Brooks, J., 1984, *The Garden Book*, Crown Publishers, New York.

Bubel, N., 1978, *The Seed Starters Handbook*, Rhodale Press, Emmaus, Pennsylvania, USA.

Cherikoff, V. & Isaacs, J. (n.d.), *The Bush Food Handbook*, Ti Tree Press, Balmain, NSW.

Clarke, G. & Toogood, A., 1992, *The Complete Book of Plant Propagation*, Ward Lock, London.

Coombes, A. J., 1998, *Eyewitness Handbooks: Trees,* Florilegium, Balmain, NSW.

Creasy, R., 1982, *The Complete Book of Edible Landscaping*, Sierra Book Club, California, USA.

Cundall, P., 1989, *The Practical Australian Gardener*, McPhee Gribble/Penguin Books, Ringwood, Victoria.

Davies, R., 1991, *Your Garden Questions Answered by Rosemary Davies*, Hyland House, Melbourne.

Department of Agriculture, New South Wales, 1981, *The Home Vegetable Garden*, NSW Department of Agriculture.

de Vaus, P., 1988, *Vegetables for Small Gardens and Containers*, Hyland House, Melbourne.

Edmanson, J., 1992, *Jane Edmanson's Working Manual for Gardeners*, Lothian Publishing Co., Melbourne.

Electricity Council, The, 1970, *Electric Growing*, The Electricity Council, London.

Fanton, M. & J., 1993, *The Seed Savers Handbook*, Seed Savers Network, Byron Bay, NSW.

Fleming, D., 1992, *Fleming's Deciduous Fruit and Ornamental Trees*, Fleming's Monbulk Nurseries, Melbourne.

Fletcher, K., 1991, *The Penguin Modern Australasian Herbal*, Penguin Books, Ringwood, Victoria.

Francis, R., 1997, *Growing Rhododendrons,* Kangaroo Press, East Roseville, NSW.

French, J., 1990, *Natural Control of Garden Pests,* Aird Books, Melbourne.

French, J., 1991, *Jackie French's Guide to Companion Planting,* Aird Books, Melbourne.

French, J., 1995, *Soil Food,* Aird Books, Melbourne.

Fryer, L. & Bradford, L., 1990, *A Child's Organic Garden,* Boolarong Publications, Brisbane.

Fukuoka, M., 1978, *The One Straw Revolution,* Rhodale Press, Emmaus, Pennsylvania, USA.

Gardiner, A., 1988, *Modern Plant Propagation,* Thomas C. Lothian, Melbourne.

Garner, R. J., 1947, *The Grafter's Handbook,* Cassell Publishers Ltd, London.

Garzoli, K., 1990, *Greenhouses* (reprint), Australian Government Publishing Service, Canberra.

Genders, R., 1969, *Mushroom Growing for Everyone,* Faber and Faber, London.

Hamilton, G., 1987, *Successful Organic Gardening,* MacMillan, Melbourne.

Hammer, P. R., 1991, *The New Topiary,* Garden Art Press, Woodbridge, UK.

Handreck, K., 1993, *Gardening Down Under,* CSIRO, Adelaide.

Hely, P. C., et al., 1982, *Insect Pests of Fruit and Vegetables in NSW,* Inkata Press, Sydney.

Hempill, J. & Hempill, R., 1991, *The Fragrant Garden,* Angus & Robertson/HarperCollins, Pymble, NSW.

Hessayon, D. G., 1985, *The Vegetable Expert,* pbi Publications, Watham Cross, UK.

Hobbs, J. & Hatch, T., 1994, *Bulbs for Gardeners and Collectors,* Florilegium, Balmain, NSW.

Hodges, J. (ed.), 1995, *The Natural Gardener: A complete guide to organic gardening,* Angus & Robertson/HarperCollins, Pymble, NSW.

Hudson, R. L., 1982, *Organic Gardening in New Zealand,* Reed Methuen Publishers, NZ.

Janson, H. F., 1996, *Pomona's Harvest,* Timber Press, Portland, Oregon, USA.

Kinsella, M. & Martindale, W. L., 1976, *Vegetables in the Home Garden* (10th ed.), Department of Agriculture, Victoria.

Lake, J., 1996, *Gardening in a Hot Climate,* Thomas C. Lothian, Melbourne.

Larkom, J., 1991, *Oriental Vegetables: The complete guide for garden and kitchen,* John Murray Publishers Ltd, London.

McLeod, J., 1994, *Heritage Gardening,* Simon & Schuster, East Roseville, NSW.

McMaugh, J., 1985, *What Garden Pest or Disease Is That?,* Lansdowne Press, Sydney.

Monfries, M. J., 1989, *Gardening in the Shade,* MacMillan, Melbourne.

Oakman, H., 1995, *Harry Oakman's What Flowers When,* University of Queensland Press, St Lucia, Queensland.

Page, P. E., 1984, *Tropical Tree Fruits for Australia,* Queensland Department of Primary Industries, Brisbane.

Phillips, R. & Rix, M., 1993, *Vegetables,* Pan Books Ltd, London.

Poincelot, R. P., 1986, *Organic No-dig, No-weed Gardening: A revolutionary method for easy gardening,* Thorson's/Rhodale Press, Emmaus, Pennsylvania, USA.

Redgrove, H. (ed.), 1991, *A New Zealand Handbook of Bulbs & Perennials*, Godwit Press Ltd, Auckland.

Rickards, P. (ed.), 1988, *A Garden Programme for Everyone*, Association for the Blind, Melbourne.

Riotte, L., 1975, *Carrots Love Tomatoes*, Storey Communications Inc., Pownal, Vermont, USA.

Rodd, Tony (chief consultant), 1999, *Botanica's Pocket Annuals & Perennials*, Random House Australia, Milsons Point, NSW.

Rodd, Tony (chief consultant), 1999, *Botanica's Pocket Trees & Shrubs*, Random House Australia, Milsons Point, NSW.

Romonowski, N., 1993, *Grasses, Bamboos and Related Plants*, Thomas C. Lothian, Melbourne.

Stephenson, W. A., 1973, *Seaweed in Agriculture and Horticulture*, E P Publishing Ltd, Wakefield, UK.

Sturgen, J., 1993, *Gardening with Containers*, Viking O'Neil, Sydney.

Sturm, J., 1992, *Complete Organic Gardening*, Southern Holdings, Huonville, Tasmania.

Sutherland, S., 1992, *Hydroponics for Everyone*, Hyland House, Melbourne.

Sutton & Sons, 1884, *The Culture of Vegetables and Flowers from Seeds and Roots*, Hamilton Adams & Co., London.

Toogood, A., 1993, *Lawn Craft*, Ward Lock, London.

Vilmorin-Andrieux, M. M., 1976, *The Vegetable Garden* (English ed.), Ten Speed Press, California, USA.

Watson, W. (ed.), 1936, *The Gardener's Assistant*, vols 1–6, The Grensham Publishing Co., London.

Whealy, K., 1994, *Seed Savers 1994 Yearbook*, Seed Savers Exchange, Decorah, Iowa, USA.

Wilkinson, J., 1993, *Bonsai Art and Technique*, Thomas C. Lothian, Melbourne.

Williams, et al., 1992, *The Complete Book of Patio and Container Gardening*, Ward Lock, London.

Wilson, E., 1999, *Worm Farm Management*, Kangaroo Press, East Roseville, NSW.

Whiteaker, S., 1985, *The Compleat Strawberry*, Century Publishing, London.

Whitten, G., 1999, *Herbal Harvest*, Blooming Books, Hawthorn, Victoria.

Wright, J. I., 1983, *Plant Propagation for the Amateur Gardener*, Blandford Press, Poole.

Yates, Arthur & Co., 1992, *Yates Garden Guide* (revised ed.), Angus & Robertson/HarperCollins, Pymble, NSW.

Yepsen, R. B. Jr (ed.), 1966, *Organic Plant Protection*, Rhodale Press, Emmaus, Pennsylvania, USA.

Further reading

Baker, Harry, 1998, *The Fruit Garden Displayed* (8th ed.), Cassell & The Royal Horticultural Society, London.

Bennett, P., 1989, *Australia and New Zealand Organic Gardening* (revised ed.), Child & Associates, Frenchs Forest, NSW.

Brickell, Christopher, 1990, *RHS's Container Gardening*, Michael Beazley Publishers, London.

Bulford, Alec, 1998, *Caring for Soil*, Kangaroo Press, East Roseville, NSW.

Clayton, S., 1994, *The Reverse Garbage Mulch Book*, Hyland House, Melbourne.

Deans, Esther, 1977, *Esther Deans' Gardening Book: Growing without digging*, Harper Row, Sydney.

Deans, Esther, 1991, *Leaves of Life: Creating therapy gardens for people with disabilities*, Angus & Robertson/HarperCollins, Pymble, NSW.

Ellis, Barbara W. & Bradley, Fern Marshall, 1996, *The Gardener's Handbook of Natural Insect and Disease Control*, Rhodale Press, Emmaus, Pennsylvania, USA.

Franck, G., 1983, *Companion Planting: Successful gardening the organic way*, Thorson's Publishing Group, Northhamptonshire, UK.

Gilbert, Allen, 1991, *Yates Green Guide to Gardening: A no fuss guide to organic gardening*, Angus & Robertson/HarperCollins, Pymble, NSW.

Gilbert, Allen, 1992, *No Garbage: Composting and recycling*, Lothian Publishing Co., Melbourne.

Gilbert, Allen, 1997, *Tomatoes for Everyone*, Hyland House, Melbourne.

Gilbert, Allen, 2000, *Climbers and Creepers*, Hyland House, Melbourne.

Gilbert, Allen, 2001, *All About Apples*, Hyland House, Melbourne.

Gilbert, Allen, 2001, *Organic Gardening for the Home Garden* (Yates Mini Guide), HarperCollins, Pymble, NSW.

Gilbert, Allen, 2001, *Trees and Shrubs for the Home Garden* (Yates Mini Guide), HarperCollins, Pymble, NSW.

Glowinski, L., 1991, *The Complete Book of Fruit Growing in Australia*, Thomas C. Lothian, Melbourne.

Jenkins, Joseph, 1999, *The Humanure Handbook: A guide to composting human manure* (2nd ed.), Chelsea Green Publishing, White River Junction, Vermont, USA.

Lanza, Patricia, 1998, *Lasagna Gardening*, Rhodale Press, Emmaus, Pennsylvania, USA.

McMaugh, Judy, 1994, *What Garden Pest or Disease Is That?: Organic and Chemical solutions for every garden problem*, New Holland Publishers (Australia) P/L, Sydney.

Mollison, B., 1991, *Introduction to Permaculture*, Tagari Publications, Sydney.

Murphy, D., 1993, *Earthworms in Australia*, Hyland House, Melbourne.

New Zealand Biodynamic Association, 1989, *Biodynamics: New directions for farming and gardening in New Zealand*, Random House New Zealand, Auckland.

Roads, M. J., 1989, *The Natural Magic of Mulch*, Greenhouse Publications, Elwood, Victoria.

Robinson, Peter, 2002, *Containers* (RHS Practical Guide), Dorling Kindersley, London.

Rosenfeld, Richard, 2002, *Herb Gardens* (RHS Practical Guide), Dorling Kindersley, London.

The Royal Horticultural Society Gardening Manual, Dorling Kindersley, London.

Stewart, Angus, 1999, *Let's Propagate: A plant propagation manual for Australia*, ABC Books, Sydney.

Thorndyke, Phoebe, 2001, *Lucky Ducks: Companions in the organic garden*, Hyland House, Melbourne.

Whiteman, Kate, 1999, *The New Guide to Fruit*, Sebastian Kelly, Oxford, UK.

Woodrow, Linda, 1996, *The Permaculture Home Garden*, Viking, Melbourne.

Index

aeration, 12, 30, 67
air plants, 86–87
almonds, 52
animal manures, 13–14, 27, 63
annuals, 53–54
ants, 69–70
aphids, 73
apple and pear scab, 75–76
apple gnome, 85–86
armillaria, 70
artichoke, Jerusalem, 47
avocado, 51

babaco, 51
bacterial gummosis, 76
bag gardens, 25, 32–33, 83
bagasse, 14
banana, 51
bark chips, 14
bathtubs, 41, 42, 68
bean rust, 74
bean shoots, growing, 82
berry fruit, 52–53
biodynamic straw, 14–15
birds, 76
   parrots and sparrows, 75
blackberries, 52
blights, fungal, 74
blood and bone, 62
blossom end rot (tomatoes), 73
blueberry, 51
boots as containers, 36
botrytis, 70
bracken fern, 45
broad beans, 48
broccoli, 48
bromeliads, 87
brown coal, 15
brown rot, 76

Brussels sprouts, 48
bulbs, 39
   propagation, 56–57

cabbage, 48
cabbage moth /butterfly, 73
cactus gardens, 27
capsicum, 48
carbon/nitrogen ratio, 5–6, 12, 13
carpets and underlays, 9, 15, 19
carrot weevil, 73
carrots, 48
cauliflower, 48
celery, 48
celery leaf spot, 73–74
chickens, 61
children's gardens, 81–87
chives, 48
chocolate spot (broad beans), 74
choko, 48
citrus gall, 76
citrus peel, dried, 16
clay soils, 7
cockchafer grubs, 74
codling moth, 76
comfrey, 45
comfrey tea, 62–63
community gardens, 87–89
companion planting, 44–46
compost and composting, 5, 13, 15
compost gardens, 23–27
compressed mulch, 15–16
concrete, camouflaging, 28
containers, feature, 36–39
copra peat, 18
corn, 48
cottage gardens, 36, 38

creeper gardens, 23
creeper lawns, 33
crop straw, 15
cubed mulch, 15–16
cucumber, 49
curl grubs, 74
currants, 53
cuttings, 54, 55–57

damping off, 70–71
diseases and pests, 68–79
   control, 97–98
drainage, 68
drying out, 10, 12, 67, 68

eelworms, 74
eggplant, 49
elderberry, 51
eucalypts
   bark and chips, 14
   leaves, 16

fertilising, 12, 25, 29, 61–65
'fish & chips,' 16
fish products, 63
French beans, 49
fruit, 50–53
fruit trees, 39–41
   pests and diseases, 69, 75–78
   pruning, 40–41
   seedlings, 40

garlic, 49
generation gardening, 7
gooseberries, 53
grape marc, 16
grass clippings, 16–17
grasshoppers, 71
gravel gardens, 27–8
green manure crops, 17

greenhouses, mini, 26, 59–60, 82, 84
grow bag gardens *see* bag gardens

hair, 17
hairy Harry, 85
hanging baskets, 38–39, 87
hardwood cuttings, 54–55
hay bales, 29–32
hazelnut, 51
heliothus caterpillar, 75
herbs, 46, 52
hessian seed mat, 33, 35
hoof and horn, 62
hot composting, 15
humus, 6
husks and shells, 17
   peanut, 19
Hydromulch, 17
hydroponic gardens, 83

illusion gardens, 86
industry by-products, 17–18

Japanese sand gardens, 27

lawns, 34
   creeper, 33
layering (garden), 5, 10–12, 13, 47
   topping up, 61–62
layering (propagation)
   aerial, 54
   ground, 57
leaf cuttings, 55
leaf miner, 78
lettuce, 49
light brown apple moth, 76–77
lime, 25
looper caterpillars, 71
lucerne, 18
lupin straw, 18

manure tea, 63
manures, animal, 13–14, 27, 63
marrows, 49
materials, 9–10, 12, 13–21
   nitrogen content, 14
mealy bug, 78
mice, 71
mineral fertilisers, 63–64
mites, 78–79
moss gardens, 28
mushroom compost, 18

nettle, stinging, 45–46
newspaper, 9–10, 18
nitrogen content of materials, 14
nitrogen draw-down, 67
nitrogen/carbon ratio, 5–6, 12, 13
no-dig gardens
   advantages, 7–8
   building, 9–12
   growth zones, 46, 47
   maintenance, 61–65
   planting techniques, 43–44
   planting zones, 47
   portable, 41
   troubleshooting, 67–79
   types, 23–42

oca, 49
onions, 49
orchards, 39–41
orchids, 86–87

palm peat, 18
paper, 18
parrots, 75
passionfruit, 51
pasture hay, 19
pawpaw, 51
pea straw, 19

peach leaf curl, 77
peanuts, 51
   shells, 19
pear and cherry slug, 77
peas, 49
pelletised mulch, 15–16
penicillium rot, 77
pepino, 51
perennials, 53–54
pests and diseases, 68–79
   control, 97–98
pine needles, 14, 16
pipe containers, 38–39
plastic bottle greenhouse, 59, 82, 84
ponds, 41–42
potatoes, 33–34, 49
   hay bale, 30, 32
   spud friends, 84–85
   spud in a bucket, 86
   tyre, 34, 35
propagating, 54–58
propagation box, 58, 59
pumpkins, 49
pyramid, portable, 26

radish, 50
recycled waste, 19
rhubarb leaf spot, 75
rock dust, 63–64
rock gardens, 27–28
rock melon, 52
rose black spot, 79

scale, 71
scarecrows, 83–84
seaweed, 19–20
   liquid fertiliser, 12, 29, 62, 64
seaweed products, 64
seed propagation, 57–59
   heat for, 26, 58–59
   sowing, 24, 44
seed saving, 58

self-propagation, 56, 87
self-seeding, 29
semi-hardwood cuttings, 55
sewage waste, 20
shells and husks, 17
   peanut, 19
shrubs and trees
  pests and diseases, 69, 78–79
silver beet, 50
silver leaf, 77
slime mould, 71
slippery mulch, 68
slugs and snails, 68, 71–72
softwood cuttings, 55
soil disturbance, 6
soil fertility, 6–7
sooty mould, 77
sparrows, 75
spinach, 50
spud friends, 84–85
spud in a bucket, 86
staghorns and elkhorns, 86
stem borers, 79

straw
  biodynamic, 14–15
  crop, 15
  lucerne and lupin, 18
  pea, 19
strawberries, 53
stumps, 36
sugar cane waste, 124

telephone books, 20
tennis court gardens, 28
toadstools, 72
toilet waste, 64
tomatoes, 50, 73
topiary, grass, 33
tree tomato, 51
trees and shrubs
  pests and diseases, 69, 78–79
turf, 34–35
tyre gardens, 34, 35–36

urea, 64–65

vegetables, 46–50
  pests and diseases, 69, 73–75
vermicast, 6, 20–21, 65
vine black spot, 77
vine downy mildew, 78
vine moth, 78

walnuts, 52
water gardens, 41–42
water propagation, 57–59
water tank gardens, 25–26
watering, 10, 68
  water-saving gardens, 27
watermelon, 52
weeds, 20, 67–68, 72
  seeds, 15, 19
white fly, 75
woodchips, 14
wool waste, 20
worm farms, 20–21
worms, 6

zucchini, 50